D1247593

SOVIET RELATIONS WITH
INDIA AND PAKISTAN

First Published in the United States, 1971
by Barnes & Noble, Inc.

ISBN 389 04196 3

Published in India by
Vikas Publications, 5 Daryaganj, Ansari Road, Delhi-6

PREFACE

THIS BOOK is an attempt to analyze the Soviet policy towards India and Pakistan, before and after the Tashkent Agreement—an important milestone on the road towards the normalization of relations between the two countries. The Soviet policy, especially after the Indo-Pakistan conflict of 1965, has been the subject of diverse speculation and controversy. The author's understanding is that the Soviet Union has shown a remarkable consistency in her attitude towards what they call the "Two Hindustan States". Even during the height of the cold war when India was, as it is now, favourably disposed towards Russia, the latter never gave up her efforts to woo Pakistan, notwithstanding Pakistan's membership of the American military pacts.

Unlike the Western Powers, the Soviet Union has looked upon the Indians and the Pakistanis as the same people—ethnically, culturally, and historically—artificially cut apart by colonialists. In the process of developing friendly relation with the two countries and strengthening the economic basis of their freedom, the Soviets have endeavoured to bring the two "blood brothers" together and help them overcome the problems left in legacy by the British rule.

The course of this twenty-three-year-old relationship has not always been quite smooth. Yet the occasional misunderstandings have been surmounted with astonishing rapidity.

It is my pleasure to acknowledge the generous help of Dr. V. S. Budhraj of Kurukshetra University in suggesting source materials. I am also thankful to the Librarian and the staff, especially Mr. Ansari, Mrs. Andrade, and Mr. Sherwani, of the Library of the Indian Council of World Affairs for their help. .

DEVENDRA KAUSHIK

CONTENTS

CHAPTER I

PRE-INDEPENDENCE TIES

THE HISTORY OF RUSSIAN RELATIONS WITH THE INDIAN subcontinent goes back to remote past. Though given a new turn by the October Revolution, it starts much earlier than 1917. Indo-Russian, Indo-Uzbek, and Indo-Armenian relations of antiquity form a rich heritage of history upon which the solid edifice of Indo-Soviet friendship has been built in our times. It is generally believed that several movements of people from Central Asia, the Caucasus and the Black Sea regions in the hoary past went into the ethnic make-up of the peoples of India and Pakistan. Strabo, a Greek historian of the 1st century BC, wrote about the flow of Indian goods along the Oxus, across the Caspian Sea, Transcaucasia and further west along the Black Sea coast.

In the 16th and 17th centuries there was considerable trade between Armenia and India.[1] A Russian account of India from the 12th or 13th century, a Slavonic translation of a Latin tale, described India as a rich country "not on fire" but "all shining in gold."[2] The first eye-witness

[1] Surendra Gopal, "Armenian Traders in India," *Central Asia*, Ed. Amalendu Guha, New Delhi, 1970, pp. 200-1.
[2] P. M. Kemp, *Bharat-Rus*, Delhi, 1948, p. 4.

account of India is, however, from the 15th century. Fifty
years before Vasco da Gama came to India a Russian
merchant from Tver, Afanasi Nikitin, travelled extensively
through the northern plains and the Deccan Plateau to
Golconda and Bijapur.

The studies conducted by Gerasim Lebedev, a talented
musician and dramatist who lived in India from 1785 to
1797, laid the foundation for a scientific study of India
in Russia. He has been rightly called the father of Russian
Indology. Lebedev knew Sanskrit and Bengali, and he
wrote Bengali dramas and staged them in Calcutta. He
was the first European translator of a Bengali classic and
the first to use European techniques for the Indian stage.[3]
Late in the 18th century the *Bhagvatgita* and *Shakun-
tala* of Kalidas were translated into Russian by a scholar
named Karamzin. In 1851, an oriental languages chair
was opened at Moscow University, and a chair of Sanskrit
at St Petersburg University in 1855.[4]

Russian Sanskritologists P. Petrov, K. Kossovich and
I. P. Minaev won renown for their scholarship. Minaev
was the first Russian orientalist to visit India, Ceylon,
Nepal, and Burma between 1874 and 1886 in order to study
Buddhism. His work, *Sketches of Ceylon and India*, is
one of the masterpieces of Russian Indology. Minaev
witnessed the first session of the Indian National Congress
held at Bombay in 1885 and hailed it in his diary as
striving for "the development of feeling of nationalism in

[3] *Russko-Indiiskie Otnosheniya V XVIII V, Cbornik Doku-
mentov*, Moscow, 1965, pp. 425-514.
[4] M. P. Babkina and S. I. Potabenko, "Soviet-Indian Cultural
Relations," *India and the Soviet Union*, Ed. V. V. Balabushevich
and Bimla Prasad, Delhi, 1969, pp. 151-2.

India, for the unification of India."[5] Minaev established close contacts with Indian orientalists and nationalist leaders like R. G. Bhandarkar, Bankim Chandra Chatterji, K. T. Telang, and Surendranath Banerjea.

The uprising of 1857 in India evoked great sympathy among the progressive circles of the Russian intelligentsia. A Russian revolutionary democrat, Dobrolyubov, wrote an article on the Indian uprising. Many Indian soldiers who deserted the British Indian Army in 1857 took shelter in Russian Central Asia after the failure of the uprising.

Settlements of Indian traders sprang up in Astrakhan, in the Volga basin, in the 17th century. From Astrakhan they supplied goods to Moscow and St Petersburg. Their request for permission to make business trips to Moscow and Petersburg was readily granted during the reign of Peter[6] the Great (1682-1725). The Tsar sent Vice-Admiral Wilster to India to sign a trade agreement with the Moghul ruler.[7] The Tsar instructed his officials to give special protection to the Indian traders settled on the Volga. They were granted temporary citizenship of Russia.[8] The Russian authorities granted Indian settlers the same rights and privileges as Russian merchants.[9] The Astrakhan colony of Indians numbered about 100. Some of them had their families with them. At the time of Napoleon's invasion of Russia, the Indian merchants contributed 30,000 roubles to the war fund of their second homeland.[10]

[5] E. Ya. Liusternik, *Russko-Indiiskie Ekonomicheskie, Nauchnie I kulturnie Sviazi V XIX V*, Moscow, 1966, pp. 146-8.
[6] *Russko-Indiiskie Otnosheniya*, pp. 52-5.
[7] *Ibid.*, p. 60.
[8] *Ibid.*, pp. 198-200.
[9] *Ibid.*, pp. 236-54.
[10] See author's article, "Materials of Indian Interest in Soviet Archives," *The Indian Archives*, Vol. XVIII, No. 1, 1969.

Central Asia provided the vital link in Russia's relations with the peoples of the Indian subcontinent. It was the region through which pilgrims and traders passed on their way to India before the discovery of the sea routes. India's political and cultural ties with the Central Asian region of the Soviet Union have indeed been very close since ancient times. In the 1st century AD North India and Central Asia formed part of a single state under Kushan rule. These political and cultural ties continued during the Middle Ages. The friendly visits of the Khwarezm scholars, Al Biruni and Abdurazak Samarkandi, form a notable chapter in the history of these contacts. Relations between the peoples of the two regions grew closer in the course of the 300-year rule of the dynasty founded by Babar.

Bukhara continued to serve as an important centre of trade and communication with India in the second half of the 19th century. Indian goods worth about 5.5 million roubles were exported to Bukhara annually.[11] Indian emigrants, numbering between 6,600 and 8,000, lived in Central Asia.[12] A great majority of them, mostly Sindhis and Punjabis, came from the western and north-western regions of India. A major portion of Indians was concentrated in the Emirate of Bukhara, the Farghana valley, Samarkand and the Syr Daria region of Turkestan. Among the Indian emigrants there were Hindus, Sikhs, and Muslims. Most of the Indians living in Central Asia were moneylenders and traders, though some peasants, craftsmen, and other working people were also present.

[11] AVPR, Sredni Aziatski Stol, 1869-1910, D., 1341; also Turkistan Vilayatining Gazeti, No. 23, 1889.
[12] For details, see G. L. Dimitriev, Iz Istorii Sredneaziatsko-Indiiskikh Otnoshenii Vtoroi Poloviny XIX-nachala XX V., Tashkent, 1965.

Trade with India suffered a setback in 1885 when the Tsarist administration imposed restrictions on Indian goods. Some concessions were, however, given to tea, muslin and indigo, and despite the restrictions Indian trade thus continued to be sizeable. Central Asia imported 700,000 pounds of tea and 18,000 pounds of indigo annually.[13] But a heavy blow was dealt to this trade in 1894 when Bukhara and Khiva were incorporated into the common tariff system of the Russian Empire. As a result Chinese tea replaced Indian, and the Peshawari tea merchants were driven out of the market.

Although trade between India and Central Asia declined because of Anglo-Russian rivalry, cultural contacts did not cease. In 1901, a branch of the Russian Society for Oriental Studies was established in Tashkent on the initiative of two Russian orientalists, A. G. Serebrenikov and A. E. Snesarev.[14] Several textbooks of Indian languages and a Russian-Hindustani dictionary were published from Tashkent. Considerable interest in Indian affairs was evinced by two important papers of Tashkent, *Turkistanskie Vedomosti*, published in Russian, and *Turkistan Vilayatining Gazeti* in Uzbek. The latter published valuable information about the visits of the Uzbek poet Furqat and traveller Said Ali Khodja to India.[15]

The national liberation movement in India felt the impact of the Russian conquest of Central Asia. It aroused in the Indian people the hope of throwing off the yoke of British colonial oppression. This hope was, however,

[13] Dokladnaya Zapiska V.O. Klemma, *O Sovremmenom Sostoianii Torgovli V Bukharskom Khanstve*, 1887.
[14] P. N. Rasulzade, *Iz Istorii Sredniaziatsko-Indiskikh Sviazei Posle Prisoedineniia Kraia K Rossii*, Tashkent, 1964, p. 16.
[15] *Turkistan Vilayatining Gazeti*, No. 20 and No. 33, 1893.

confined in the beginning to a few rulers of princely states who had no popular aspirations and simply sought to exploit the contradictions between the two colonial powers to their advantage.

In November 1865, soon after the incorporation of Tashkent into the Tsarist Empire, Maharaja Ranbir Singh of Kashmir sent his emissaries there to seek Russian aid against the British. But the mission did not meet with success.[16] The Tsarist Government was not interested in promoting the cause of the national liberation of India. It was interested only in its own colonial expansion, and for want of adequate material resources did not at that moment feel inclined to involve itself in trouble with the powerful British Empire. In 1866, the ruler of Indore sent a mission to Tashkent with the same object, but this too met a similar fate. A second mission from Maharaja Ranbir Singh reached Tashkent in 1870, but again no political or military help was promised. It was natural for the Indian princes and people to seek help from any quarter, but it is doubtful whether the aid of colonial Russia, if given at all, would have led to the real liberation of the country. Tsarist Russia — the "gendarme of European reaction" and the "prison of nations," could hardly be expected to act out of altruistic motives.

The mission of Guru Charan Singh, who arrived in Tashkent in 1879, may be described as the first popular mission. He was sent by the Namdhari Sikhs of Punjab who wished to liberate the province from British rule. Guru Charan Singh, who undertook this hazardous journey in his seventies, tried to impress on the Russian authorities

---

[16] For a detailed account, see N. A. Khalfin's paper, *Indian Missions in Russia in the Second Half of the 19th Century,* XXVI International Congress of Orientalists, Moscow, 1963.

the need to help the Indian people in their struggle for national liberation. Writing about the mission, N. A. Ivanov, chief of the Zeravshan district, stressed the "importance of the fact that a part of the population of British India appealed to us to help liberate them from the foreign yoke" and noted that "in the speeches of Guru Charan Singh we find such confidence in Russia's power, such belief that we were destined to liberate the Indian people from the hateful domination of Britain, that it is impossible to doubt our great moral impact on the population of British India."[17] But again the Government turned a deaf ear to the request of the Indian patriot. The Governor-General of Turkestan, Gen Kaufmann, gave a non-committal reply couched in friendly language.

Although no concrete help was received from Russia by the national liberation movement in India through these missions, their despatch nevertheless indicated that the Indian people had built high hopes upon Russian aid in their struggle. The visit of Russian warships to Bombay in 1879 created a popular stir. People rushed to the city to convince themselves of the presence of the ships and "began to talk of a quick downfall of the British yoke, which would be cast off by Russia and Nana Sahib," the *Times of India* wrote on 19 May the same year.

Another significant indication of the hopes Indian patriots pinned on Russian aid is provided by Tilak's overtures to the Russian consuls in Bombay, Tcherkin and Klemm. Tilak is reported to have sought Russian help in sending Indian youths abroad for military training. He also approached them for introductions to Russian firms in order to purchase machinery for the establishment of

[17] *Ibid.*

factories in India.[18]

The disinclination of Tsarist Russia to render aid to the Indian people explodes the myth of the "Russian meance" to India. This clearly shows it was an invention of the British to cover up their own intended aggression in Central Asia. The Russian bogey was also used by the British rulers of India to prevent the development of friendly contacts with the Russian people.

But the Indian people never accepted the British canard about the danger to the security of India from Russia even during the period before the October Revolution. Peter the Great's will, which is often cited as evidence of a Russian plan to conquer India, is considered by historians a false document, and the orders given by the mad Tsar Paul for invasion of India in 1801, which did not have even the remotest chance of being executed, were rescinded by his successor. In fact, an invasion of India was highly impracticable in view of the military weakness of Russia, the political conditions in that country and the enormous problems of economic and transport it would have involved.

A perusal of the proceedings of the Indian National Congress in its early years shows how strongly it opposed British proposals for increased military expenditure on the pretext of counteracting the Russian threat to India's security.[19] The Congress opposed the "forward policy" on the northwest frontier. At its seventh Session in 1891 Dinshaw Wacha refuted the government's assertion that this policy stemmed from the Russian advance in Central Asia.

[18] Source Material for a History of the Freedom Movement in India, II, pp. 215-16.

[19] Bimal Prasad, The Origins of Indian Foreign Policy, Calcutta, 1960, pp. 37-44.

Wacha accused the British Government in India of having "initiated aggression under one pretext or another." He declared: "Russia only responds to the British move. Outpost answers outpost and gun answers gun." He called for a complete reversal of the "forward policy," which he described as "an unwise and aggressive policy which, under the hollow pretext of defending the empire, secretly aims at extending its frontier."[20]

The British in India continued to harp on the bogey of Russian advance even after the overthrow of Tsarist rule. As Jawaharlal Nehru wrote:

We have grown up in the tradition, carefully nurtured by England, of hostility to Russia. For long years past the bogey of a Russian invasion has been made the excuse of vast expenditure on our armaments. In the days of the Tsars we were told that the imperialism of Russia was for ever driving south, coveting an outlet to the sea, or may be India itself. The Tsar has gone but the rivalry between England and Russia continues and we are now told that India is threatened by the Soviet Government.[21]

With the October Revolution relations between the Russian and Indian peoples entered a qualitatively new phase. If Tsarist Russia had snubbed all the efforts of Indian revolutionaries and patriots to forge a link with it, the Soviet power readily welcomed all such Indians as wished to work for the liberation of India from British rule and openly espoused the cause of all oppressed peoples of the East. The Soviets declared their opposition to all forms of colonialism.

[20] Report of the Seventh Indian National Conference, pp. 28-36.
[21] J. Nehru, Soviet Russia, 1928, p. 191.

Early Soviet documents such as the Declaration of the Rights of the Peoples of Russia, Appeal to All the Working Muslims of Russia and of the East, and a series of other acts proclaimed the principles of the Leninist policy of friendship with the colonial peoples of Asia and made a great impact upon freedom-fighters in India and elsewhere.

The October Revolution influenced the Indian freedom struggle in many important ways despite the wide ideological gap which separated these two movements. It contributed to a quickening of the pace of the national struggle in India and helped broaden the base of that struggle by drawing into it industrial workers and organized peasantry and youth. Even the official Indian Constitutional Reform Report published in 1918 was forced to admit that "it [the October Revolution] has given an impetus to Indian political aspirations."[22] The revolution gave social content and a progressive world outlook to the freedom movement in India.

How greatly the British rulers of India were alarmed, by the Leninist Declaration of Rights of the Peoples of Russia (16 November 1917) and the Appeal of the Council of People's Commissars to all Muslim Toilers of Russia and the East (20 November 1917), is revealed by some documents preserved in the National Archives of India. The Secretary of State for India in his telegram to the Viceroy of India, dated 7 December 1917, said: We have held up highly inflammatory proclamation by Bolsheviks addressed to all labouring class of Moslems of

[22] Report on the Indian Constitutional Reform, HMSO, Cmd. 9109, p. 14.

Russia and the East transmitted by Russian Government Wirless. It should be suppressed as long as possible.

The British authorities took "all possible steps to hold up telegrams at Peking, Tokyo, Washington, and in Dutch East Indies," though they felt that "it will probably leak out eventually." They were considering measures to "counterblast" it and "warning local officers of possible publication" of the Appeal to Muslim Toilers signed by Lenin. The British Government of India described the proclamation of Lenin about the independence of nations as "diabolical." The Secretary of State suggested to the Viceroy that the despatch of "strong telegrams from prominent Indian Mohammedans" be organized to Baku and and Tbilisi refuting the stories of oppression of Muslims in India. The Aga Khan was approached by the Secretary of State while the Nizam of Hyderabad was left to be tackled by the Viceroy. As already noted, despite the British cordon, information about Lenin's proclamations on self-determination found its way into India. Lenin's famous Decrees on Peace and Land and his Declaration of Rights of the Peoples of Russia and Appeal to Muslim Toilers of Russia and the the East were frequently referred to quite enthusiastically and admiringly by many prominent Indian writers and public figures.[23]

Lenin and India

Lenin was not only the leader of victorious socialism but also the most ardent champion of national revolutions. Lenin's interest in the national revolutions of the colonial

[23] See Devendra Kaushik, Leonid Mitrokhin (Eds.) *Lenin— His Images in India*, Delhi, 1970, pp. IX-X.

countries antedates the October Revolution and the establishment of the Comintern. In fact, Lenin was the first Marxist to make a deep theoretical analysis of the new stage of the 20th century national revolutionary movements. References to India in Lenin's works occur from the fourth volume of the *Collected Works* to almost the last—from 1900 to 1923.

Lenin's interest in the national revolutions of colonial countries was genuine and rooted in principle. He did not consider his work finished with the founding of the first socialist state, and he created the Communist International to promote the world socialist revolution and ensure the victory of the national liberation movement. Lenin submitted his thesis on the Colonial and National Question to the Second Congress of the Comintern in 1920 outlining the character, strategy and tactics and perspective of national revolutions in the colonial world.

Along with Lenin's theses the Second Congress also endorsed M.N. Roy's supplementary thesis on the subject. Roy wrote that after reading his draft Lenin "suggested some verbal alterations which I readily accepted."[24] This was, however, not true.

Soviet scholars have recently published the full text of Roy's original draft, as also the deletions and changes made by Lenin in his own handwriting which show that the changes were quite substantial and material.

In the original draft, in his seventh thesis, Roy had written:

The revolutionary movements in the colonies are essentially an economic struggle. The bourgeois demo-

[24] M. N. Roy, *Memoirs*, p. 381.

cratic nationalist movements are limited to the small middle class which does not reflect the aspirations of the masses. Without the active support of the masses, the national freedom of the colonies will never be attained. But in many countries, especially in India, the masses are not with the bourgeois nationalist leaders—they are moving towards revolution independently of the bourgeois nationalist movement.

...but it would be a mistake to assume that the bourgeois nationalist movement expresses the sentiments and aspirations of the general population.

...but the Communist International must not find in them the media through which the revolutionary movements in the colonies should be helped. The mass movements in the colonies are growing independently of the nationalist movements. The masses distrust the political leaders who always lead them astray and prevent them from revolutionary action.[25]

All the above sentences were deleted by Lenin. His own views were just the opposite and he held that the Communists of the East "will have to base themselves on the bourgeois nationalism that is awakening in these peoples, cannot but awaken, and has historical justification." Lenin considered that nationalism of the oppressed peoples, in so far as it was directed against imperialism, had a progressive revolutionary content.

[25] G. Adhikari, "Lenin on Roy's Supplementary Colonial Theses," Marxist Miscellany, Delhi, 1970, pp. 1-30; also see A. Reznikov, "Lenin on the National Liberation Movement" and "Lenin's Struggle against Sectarian Distortions in the National Colonial Question," Kommunist, No. 7, 1967 & No. 5, 1968.

Roy desired the anti-colonial revolutions to develop as class revolutions, but Lenin inscribed on the banner of the Comintern the slogan, "Workers of all Countries and all Oppressed Peoples Unite."

Lenin looked at the socialist movement of capitalist countries and the national movement of the colonial countries as interrelated and interdependent and worked for their alliance.

On the contrary, Roy counterposed the socialist movement of capitalist countries to the national movement and went in for vulgar idealization of the role of the worker-peasant masses without taking into consideration the actual level of their class consciousness and organization. Lenin, on the other hand, realized that class consciousness would grow out of a vibrant, anti-imperialist national consciousness. He mapped out the concept of a united anti-imperialist national front. It is an irony of history that an Indian should have opposed it.

These differences between Roy and Lenin on the questions of strategy and tactics of the struggle of the colonial peoples led to a widely divergent evaluation of Gandhi and his role.

Gandhi's views and activities have long been an object of study in the USSR. Articles and informative materials devoted to him started appearing in Soviet magazines in the early 1920s. It is noteworthy that A. V. Lunacharsky, People's Commissar for Education, was one of the first to write a special article on Gandhi in 1923. Roy has written that Chicherin, People's Commissar for Foreign Affairs, also had a positive evaluation of Gandhi's role. Zhizn Natsional-nostei (Journal of the Commissariat of Nationalities), headed by Stalin, published an article on Gandhi in its fourth issue of 1921 highlighting his influence on the masses.[26] Surits, Soviet Ambassador to Afghanistan, also spoke of Gandhi approvingly.

It would be wrong to think that Gandhi was never looked upon with respect and understanding by the Soviet scholars. Of course, in the later works by A. M. Dyakov, V. V. Balabushevich, E. Zhukov, and I. M. Reisner a rather onesided and largely negative appraisal of Gandhi was made. But the reason for this also lay in the complexity of Gandhi's world outlook, contradictions in some of his practical actions as well in the lack at that time of data for a thorough and all-round investigation of Gandhi's activities. Moreover, even for many ardent Gandhians, including Nehru, some of his actions abounded in such unexpected turns that at times they were quite surprised. Nehru characterized them as the "paradoxes" of Gandhi.

In his reminiscences, Roy writes that Lenin looked upon Gandhi as a recognized leader of the national liberation movement in India: "The role of Gandhi was the crucial point of difference. Lenin believed that as the inspirer and leader of a mass movement he was a revolutionary. I maintained that a religious and cultural revivalist, he was bound to be socially reactionary, however revolutionary he might appear politically."[27]

Lenin continued to follow with interest Gandhi's activities as leader of the movement for Indian freedom. In January 1922, he started making preparations for the article, "Notes of a Publicist," which unfortunately remained unfinished. There is a thesis in the plan which Lenin drew up for this article. Lenin wrote: "Two fronts and the

[26] The bulletin of the Commissariat of External Affairs, *Biulletin NKID*, No. 65, 1921, also carried an appreciative article on Gandhi.
[27] M. N. Roy, op. cit., p. 379.

middle; Hindu-Tolstoyan." The Soviet scholar, P. Shastiko, thinks that by "Hindu-Tolstoyan" Lenin meant Gandhi.[28] Gandhi, as is known, had corresponded with Tolstoy in 1909 from South Africa and translated his "Letter to a Hindu."

Lenin's study in the Kremlin contains a copy of issue No. 19 of the magazine, *Communist International* (17 December 1921). An article, "The Present Situation in India" (it has not been possible to ascertain its authorship), in this issue, appraised favourably the non-violent struggle conducted by Gandhi in India.

On 14 February 1921, Lenin received Abdurab, a leader of the Indian Revolutionary Association in Tashkent.[29] The contents of their talk are not known to us as they were not recorded. But from a list of books on the Indian national movement subsequently sent by Abdurab to Lenin on 16 February it is evident they discussed the Indian movement. The next day he instructed his secretary to send the list to L. B. Krasin, then negotiating a trade agreement with Britain in London, to obtain copies. Among the 35 books which aroused Lenin's interest there were *The Life and Speeches of Gandhi* and other works.[30]

Lenin, already bedridden, turned his attention for the last time to India in his article, "Better Fewer, But Better," written on 2 March 1923. With great optimism Lenin wrote:

[28] P. Shastiko, "Lenin and Gandhi," *Soviet Review*, New Delhi, Vol. VI, No. 72, 30 September 1969.

[29] For details of the activities of Indian revolutionaries, see author's article, "Indian Revolutionaries in Soviet Asia," *Link*, 26 January 1966.

[30] For further details, see author's article, "About the Founding of the Communist Party of India at Tashkent," *New Age* (monthly), October 1964.

In the last analysis, the outcome of the struggle will be determined by the fact that Russia, India, China, etc., account for the overwhelming majority of the population of the globe. And during the past few years it is this majority that has been drawn into the struggle for emancipation with extraordinary rapidity, so that in this respect there cannot be the slightest doubt what the final outcome of the world struggle will be. In this sense, the complete victory of socialism is fully and absolutely assured.

Lenin was prevented by his preoccupation with internal Soviet affairs — the rampant civil war and foreign intervention and the awful famine — and his own deteriorating health from devoting as much attention to the national revolution in India and other colonial countries as he had desired. It is unfortunate that the correct line on the colonial question as laid down by Lenin was changed for a dogmatic, sectarian line adopted at the Sixth Congress of the Comintern in 1928. This resulted in the isolation of the parties of the working class from the national movement, with consequent harm to the cause of social revolution in the colonial countries.

This erroneous course of policy was corrected at the Seventh Comintern Congress in 1935. Yet all the necessary correctives were not effected by a self-critical evaluation of the negative course followed between the Sixth and the Seventh Congress, and only the tactical character of the change was stressed, which allowed an easy relapse into the anti-Leninist ideological posture after the end of the World War II.

The significance of the disintegration of the colonial empires in which the Soviet Union had played a decisive

role by defeating fascism was missed and the independence
of newly liberated countries like India was dubbed a sham.
It was only much later, in 1956 at the Twentieth Congress
of the CPSU and subsequently at the Moscow Conferences
of Communist Parties in 1957 and 1960, that the correct
Leninist ideological stand towards national revolutions was
restored.

A frank and honest admission of the mistakes, however,
does not mean that the Comintern was only an instrument
to promote the narrow national interests of the Soviet
Union and that the Soviet role in the process of breakup
of the colonial system was not crucial.[31]

[31] Indian scholar Zafar Imam has argued that the Soviet attitude towards the colonial problem was not motivated by "philan-
thropic consideration." Rather, it was a "skilful exercise in
realpolitik," with its numerous shifts and balances effected to
suit the changing needs of the Soviet leitmotiv towards Britain.
He holds that after Lenin's death and with the rise of Stalin the
national interest of the Soviet state was gradually made the
determining factor of the Soviet attitude towards Britain. (Colonialism in East-West Relations, A Study of Soviet Policy Towards
India and Anglo-Soviet Relations, 1917-1947, New Delhi, 1969, pp.
481-2.) The writer, while conceding Soviet Union's "deep interest" in the breakup of colonialism, which "in the ultimate
analysis did exercise a remarkable influence on the whole process"
and acted as a "catalyst" in raising the tempo of Indian national
movement, concludes that no "concrete action" was taken by the
Soviet power against British imperialism in India.
    Another Indian scholar, Harish Kapur, though he did not make
a case study of India, has made the general observation that
Soviet policy towards the colonial world was "revolutionary and
relatively straightforward." Kapur writes: "Despite many tactical
fluctuations, its basic and permanent objective was to extend open
support to the various nationalistics forces, help them both
morally and materially to become independent of European control." (Soviet Russia and Asia, 1917-1927, Geneva, 1965.)
    K. P. S. Menon holds that "the Russian Revolution unques-
tionably hastened the disintegration of Europe's colonial empire
and her political influence on other parts of the world." (Lenin
Through Indian Eyes, Delhi, 1970, pp. 26-7.)

Lack of contradiction between the interests of the world socialist revolution and national liberation movements and the interests of the first workers and peasants state is not just a product of Marxist semantics. It is a historical truth that the strength of the Soviet Union has acted as the most dependable bulwark of national liberation movements against imperialism. Soviet legions might not have come to India to liberate her from British rule, but there is no gainsaying the fact that the October Revolution marked the first breach in the citadel of imperialism, and the victory of Soviet arms against fascism and the growth of a world socialist camp created the objective conditions for India and other Afro-Asian countries to win freedom.

Mistakes in the evaluation of the role of the colonial bourgeoisie need not be attributed to the so-called resurgence of nationalism in Soviet Russia, nor can a desire to come to terms with British imperialism be seen in them. With the inner party struggle in the Soviet Union and the betrayal of the Chinese revolution by the national bourgeoisie, the ultra-left sectarian assessment of the national bourgeoisie in India by Indian representatives in the Comintern (Roy in the Second Congress, and Shaukat Usmani and Saumendranath Tagore in the Sixth Congress) must take the blame for these distortions of the Leninist line.[32]

---

[32] J. A. Naik says the Sixth Congress line was of "Russian origin," (op. cit., p. 21.) The Indian delegates to the Sixth Congress, Usmani and Tagore, however, outdid everybody in denigrating Gandhi and the nationalist movement, whereas Kuusinen, who delivered the report on the colonial question, cautioned against treating the Indian National Congress as a "common counter-revolutionary party" despite its betrayal of anti-imperialist struggle in 1922. Kuusinen called Nehru a "national revolutionary" and referred to his participation in the Anti-imperialist League and visit to Moscow. He spoke admiringly of

The Draft Programme adopted at the Sixth Congress
of the Comintern had not ruled out "temporary agreements
with the national bourgeoisie" provided such agreements
did not hamper the revolutionary organization of the
workers and peasants. But even this cautious formulation
met the opposition of the Indian delegate, Narayan
(Saumendranath Tagore), who in his speech held that
"the bourgeoisie can never fight imperialism genuinely."[33]

Some critics of Soviet policy towards India during
British rule even accuse Lenin of having struck a "judicis
ous (or revolutionary) compromise" between "a policy of
active hostility towards Britain's imperialist interests and
the need for reaching a *modus vivendi* with Britain." This
policy, they further allege, degenerated after Lenin's death
into the well-defined purpose of safeguarding the Soviet
state and also strengthening its hands in arriving at a
rapprochement with the capitalist powers.[34]

To prove Lenin's "compromising" attitude towards
British imperialism, the failure of the Third Congress of
the Comintern to discuss the colonial question is often
cited. It is also alleged that the Comintern did not pay
enough attention to the Indian and colonial question because of the prohibition clause of the Anglo-Russian Trade
Agreement of March 1921 concerning propaganda. The
Third Congress did not hold a detailed discussion on the
colonial question as only the previous year it had had a

---

the peasant action organized by the Congress in Bardoli in 1928
(*International Press Correspondence*, Vol. 8, No. 81, 21 November 1928, p. 1525).

[33] *International Press Correspondence*, Vol. 8, No. 66, 25
September. 1928, p. 1203.

[34] Zafar Imam, *op. cit.*, pp. 46, 481; Helene Carrere d'Encausse
and Stuart R. Schram, *Marxism and Asia*, London, 1969, pp. 40-2
(English translation).

long debate on it.

Roy was naturally upset, for he desired to attack the Leninist line and change it. But the absence of discussion had nothing to do with the clause on propaganda. Just about the same time the Soviet leaders were holding discussions with a large group of Indian revolutionaries whom they had invited from Berlin. As for the closure of the Tashkent Military School for Indians, the main reason was internal bickerings between rival Indian groups.[35]

Moreover, Lenin had from the very beginning serious misgivings about Roy's plan to organize a liberation army on the northwest frontier of India. The uncooperative attitude of Afghanistan was also a big hurdle. Yet, because of his tremendous sympathy for the cause of Indian liberation, Lenin gave a free hand to Roy to execute his plans. Lenin laid great stress on preparing revolutionary ideological programme and organization before resorting to armed struggle. In this sphere the Soviet Union continued to assist without loudly proclaiming its note.

The trade agreement, of 1921 notwithstanding, the Soviet regime supported the anti-imperialist struggles of the colonial peoples. Comintern journals and magazines continued to carry anti-British articles. Lord Curzon, within six months of his assuming office as Foreign Secretary, delivered a virtual ultimatum on 8 May 1923, to Moscow threatening to terminate trade relations unless the Soviet Government stopped its anti-British propaganda and withdrew its "agents" from India, Afghanistan, and Persia. But the Soviets were not deterred by such threats. The Fourth Congress of the Comintern passed a thesis on the Eastern Question, which called upon Communists to

[35] For a detailed account, see author's article, "Indian Revolutionaries in Soviet Asia," Link, 26 January 1966.

organize trade unions in the colonial countries and cooperate with bourgeois agencies struggling for national
liberation.[36] The Congress also sent a telegram of greetings
to the All-India Trade Union Congress reminding the
Indian Communists of their twofold task: to fight for
improved "conditions" for the workers and for "national
political freedom."[37]

The Fourth Congress stated in its Thesis on the Eastern
Question:

> ... the Communist International supports every
> national revolutionary movement against imperialism....
> In the conditions prevailing in the West ... the slogan
> put forward is that of the proletarian united front, but
> in the Colonial East the slogan that must be emphasised
> at the present time is that of the anti-imperialist united
> front.... The danger of an agreement between bour-
> geois nationalism and one or several rival imperialist
> powers is far greater in the semi-colonial countries like
> China or Persia, or in the countries which are fighting
> for their independence by exploiting inter-imperialist
> rivalries like Turkey, than it is in the colonies.[38]

The Fifth Congress, which met in June-July 1924,
issued a manifesto supporting the revolutionary movements of the peoples of the East. The congress recommended in a resolution that the Executive Council of the

---

[36] J. Degras (Ed.), *The Communist International, Documents*,
London, 1956, Vol. 1, pp. 382-93. According to Sir C. Kaye,
Ranjan Das (the son of C. R. Das) and Subhas Chandra Bose
were among the five Indians to whom invitations to attend
the Fourth Congress had been issued (*Communism in India*,
pp. 272-8).

[37] *Ibid.*, pp. 393-4.

[38] J. Degras, *op. cit.*, pp. 385 and 390.

Communist International should expand "direct contact" with the "national movements for emancipation."[39] Obviously, the intention, so far as it applied to India, was to establish direct relations between the Executive Council and the Indian National Congress. But Roy opposed this completely and suggested "direct connection with the masses."[40]

Roy had a difficult time at the Fifth Congress while trying to challenge the Leninist line. The chairman of the Colonial Commission, Manuilsky, charged Roy with deviationism:

> Some deviations were recorded by the commission. Roy, as at the Second Congress, exaggerated the social movement in the colonies to the detriment of the national movement.... He goes so far as to say that the national movement had lost its character of the united front of all the classes of an oppressed country, that a new period was beginning, in which the class struggle was becoming transported into the colonies.... In regard to the colonial question, Roy reflects the nihilism of Rosa Luxemburg. The truth is that a just proportion should be looked for between the social movement and the national movement. Can the right of self-determination become a contradiction to the interest of the revolution? Had Roy put the question in this manner, one could discuss it with him.[41]

Thus Roy's attempts at changing the right Leninist course of the Comintern on the colonial question failed

[39] J. Degras, op. cit., Vol. II, pp. 156-9.
[40] International Press Correspondence, Vol. 4, 25 July 1924, pp. 518-19.
[41] International Press Correspondence, Vol. 4, No. 57, 12 August 1924, p. 608.

up to the Fifth Congress. Though Roy was absent at the next Congress, his views were amply represented through other diehard dogmatists from India. It is also somewhat ironical that when the Sixth Congress adopted more or less his viewpoint, Roy, chastened by experience, changed it. All this sowed great confusion and caused irreparable damage to relations between Moscow and the national movement in India.

That the Indian people and their leaders, by and large, retained their friendly feelings towards the Soviet Union, despite its occasionally rigid attitude, as reflected in the sectarian line adopted at the Sixth Congress, can only be explained by their deep conviction about the anti-imperialist character of the Soviet power. When Nazi Germany invaded the Soviet Union in 1941 the Indian people and their leaders strongly condemned it and extended their full moral support to the heroic struggle against fascist aggression. As the war drew to an end, Nehru noted the clear distinction between British and Soviet war aims in *Discovery of India*. He contrasted Churchill's brazen-faced declaration about the non-applicability of the Atlantic Charter to India with Stalin's declaration of Soviet war aims.[42]

[42] J. Nehru, *Discovery of India*, Calcutta, 1946, pp. 397-8.

CHAPTER II

MISTY DAWN : EARLY
SOVIET ATTITUDE, 1947-52

EXPRESSING THE THOUGHTS OF HIS COLLEAGUES IN THE
Congress as well as his own about the example of other
nations which they would like a future independent India
to follow, Jawaharlal Nehru wrote in Ahmednager Fort
prison in 1944.

We thought of the United States of America and even
of some eastern countries which were forging ahead.
But most of all we had the example of the Soviet Union
which in two brief decades, full of war and civil strife
and in the face of what appeared to be insurmountable
difficulties, had made tremendous progress. Some were
attracted to communism, others were not, but all were
fascinated by the advance of the Soviet Union
in education and culture and medical care and physical
fitness and in the solution of the problem of nationali-
ities—by the amazing and pordigious effort to create a
new world out of the dregs of the old.[1]

As Vice-President of the Interim Government of India,

[1] J. Nehru, The Discovery of India, pp. 394-5.

Nehru declared at his first press conference on 7 September 1946, that it would be the policy of his government to build up good relations with both the Great Powers—the Soviet Union and the United States. In his very first statement he outlined free India's non-aligned policy, maintaining that it would try "to keep away from the power politics of groups aligned against one another, which have led in the past to world wars and which may again lead to disaster on an even vaster scale."[2] He conveyed his country's greetings to the Soviet Union in these words:

> To that other great nation of the modern world, the Soviet Union, which also carries a vast responsibility for shaping world events, we send greetings. They are our neighbours in Asia and inevitably we shall have to undertake many common tasks and have much to do with each other.[3]

In December 1946 the Indian Science Congress invited Soviet scientists to visit India at the instance of Nehru. The USSR Academy of Sciences sent a delegation of four scientists with academician V. P. Volgin as its leader. Back home, Volgin gave an interview to *Izvestia* and spoke of the Indian visit as having "left a great impression" on the Soviet scientists. "Everyone we met in India," Volgin stated in *Izvestia* of 2 February 1947, "showed a vital interest in the accomplishments of the Soviet Union and the livesliest joy at the arrival of the representatives of Soviet culture."

India established diplomatic ties with the Soviet Union on 13 April 1947. A press communique issued in New Delhi said the two governments had agreed to exchange

[2] *The Statesman*, 8 September 1946.
[3] *Ibid*.

diplomatic missions at the level of ambassador. The first
Indian Ambassador to the Soviet Union was appointed on 25 June 1947. On Nehru's instructions, the first
step of sounding the Soviet Union about the establishment of diplomatic relations had been taken much earlier.
V. K. Krishna Menon and K. P. S. Menon met Soviet
Foreign Minister, M. Molotov, in Paris on 28 September
1946, for this purpose. Molotov welcomed the idea.

The appointment of an Indian Ambassador before the
country was partitioned meant technically that the appointment was made on behalf of the whole of India,
including those areas which later separated to form Pakistan. Diplomatic relations between Pakistan and the
Soviet Union were, however, established much later. On
2 May 1948, Tass announced that both governments had
agreed to exchange diplomatic missions. The Pakistan
Government opened an embassy in Moscow on 30 October 1949 and the Soviet Union announced the appointment of an ambassador to Pakistan three weeks later.
But the Ambassador arrived in Pakistan only in March
1950.[4]

According to K. P. S. Menon, relations between India
and the Soviet Union after independence may be divided
into two phases—one passive phase and the other active.
The active phase, in his opinion, began in 1955.[5] A period
of transition may be marked from 1953 to 1955. In fact,
a slow change can be discerned towards the end of 1952
and early 1953, in the last days of Stalin.

The establishment of diplomatic ties between India

[4] Sangat Singh, Pakistan's Foreign Policy, Bombay, 1970,
p. 129.
[5] News and Views from the Soviet Union, New Delhi, No.
3, 1961.

and the USSR did not lead to an immediate development of close economic and cultural relations. There were many psychological barriers to be crossed. "Some Indians," wrote K. P. S. Menon, "still suffered from the fear, relic of British days, that the USSR was out to turn the world red by hook or crook; and many Russians thought that though India was nominally free, she was economically bound hand and foot to the chariot of Western imperialism."[6]

The preoccupation of the Soviet Union with its own postwar problems—rehabilitation of a devastated economy and the threat to her security from the cold war unleashed by the Western Powers—prevented Moscow from giving enough attention to developing relations with the newly independent countries.

When India and Pakistan became independent the Soviet leaders failed to grasp the significance of this historic development. In most of the Soviet writings of this period both states were treated as Anglo-American colonies. The existence of foreign capital in the two states and their continuation in the British Commonwealth of Nations was considered a proof of their vassal status. The fact that the Governor-General of India and the chiefs of the armed forces in both India and Pakistan, several governors of provinces, and a host of other high civil, military and diplomatic officials were Britons baffled the Soviet leaders.

The ban imposed on the exhibition of Soviet films, refusal of the Indian Government to issue visas to Soviet delegates to the All-India Students' Federation Conference, prohibition of the Conference of Progressive Writers

[6] K. P. S. Menon, *Lenin Through Indian Eyes*, Delhi, 1970, pp. 67-8.

in May 1949, in which delegates of the Soviet Writers'
Association were to participate, refusal of the Pakistan
Government to allow Pakistani writers to visit the USSR
on the 33rd anniversary of the October Revolution in
1950, and the coolness shown by Liaquat Ali Khan, Prime
Minister of Pakistan, to the invitation to visit the USSR
in 1949, which he used to extract an invitation from
Washington—all these incidents affected early Soviet attitude to India and Pakistan. This attitude was already
cautious, thanks to the reversal of the correct course outlined by the Seventh Comintern Congress in 1935, and a
slide back into the un-Leninist sectarian line of the Sixth
Congress facilitated by the cold-war atmosphere.

Lack of direct contact between the Soviet Union and
India for a long time also produced many of the misunderstandings of the early period. Until the Soviet Union
entered the Second World War in 1941, no Soviet
national had openly visited the Indian subcontinent.
Shortly after, however, Soviet representatives visited Calcutta and one or two other industrial centres to buy war
material. The first Soviet resident in India was perhaps
Gladyshev, a Tass correspondent who came in the summer
of 1942.[7]

Relations with Pakistan

Despite delay in establishing diplomatic relations, for
which partly the mental reservations of the League leaders
towards the Soviet Union were responsible, economic and
cultural relations between the two states did unexpectedly
well once diplomatic missions were opened. Indeed, there
was an exchange of cultural, medical, and trade groups

[7] T. G. P. Spear's article on "Soviet Publications on India,"
Central Asian Review, Vol. 5, No. 1, 1957.

even before the establishment of formal state relations. In 1949, a Russian trade group arrived in Pakistan, followed by a group of Soviet doctors in 1951. In 1952, a Pakistani cultural group visited the USSR. Soviet journalists attended a conference in Karachi. Between 1948 and 1952 Pakistan's trade with the Soviet Union increased. In 1952, exports to that country rose sharply to 10 per cent of Pakistan's exports. But the next year saw a marked decline, bringing this figure down to 4 per cent.[8] In September 1952, a barter contract for 150,000 tons of Russian wheat in exchange for 22,000 tons of jute and 13,150 tons of cotton was signed in Karachi.[9]

Some Soviet ideological opposition to the partition of India and to the Muslim League which sponsored this demand, existed, though this did not prevent the establishment of relations between the two countries. This can be seen in the writings of the leading Soviet Indologist Dyakov, who in his book, *Natsional'nyy Vopros I Angliyskiy Imperializm V Indii* (Moscow, 1948), described the principle of "divide and rule" as the cornerstone of British policy in India and called the Muslim League a tool of the British from its inception (p.189). Dyakov accused the League leaders of "demagogy," through which "they managed to attract fairly wide masses of the Muslim democratic intelligentsia and of the Muslim peasantry" (p.38).

But to be fair to Dyakov, it should be noted that he was equally critical of the Hindu Mahasabha. He wrote: "The organisation which in the eyes of the British ruling circles was to undermine the Congress influence among the Hindus and to complete the split of the national-

---

[8] J. A. Murphy, *Pakistan-Soviet Relations*, a Columbia University thesis, pp. 32-3 (microfilmed).
[9] *Ibid.*

liberation movement was the Hindu Mahasabha" (p.39). Nor did Dyakov spare the princes for acting as tools of British imperialism. He observed: "It would be incorrect to think that British imperialism relied only on the Muslim landowners and compradore bourgeoisie. The princes, who are even now the firmest supportes of British imperialism, are mostly Hindus."

Dyakov wrote that though the Indian National Congress was not a communal organization, its members were mostly Hindus because of certain "peculiarities of the development of capitalism in India." "The weak Muslim representation gave the party... a fairly sharply defined Hindu colouring. ... Muslim communal leaders and British ruling circles widely used these facts to estrange the Muslim masses from the National Congress." He was also critical of the Congress for not making "serious attempts to win support among the Muslim masses" and described the party's programme as "insufficiently radical to attract the Muslim masses."

In his later work, *India Vo Vremiy I Posle Vtoroi Mirovoi Voiny, 1939-49* (Moscow, 1952), Dyakov called Pakistan an "artificial state" and commented that the "sole link" between its two parts was "a common religion" (p.129). On the basis of these remarks, some writers have hastened to describe Pakistan as a state which did not "fit into Marxist ideology." A remark by Stalin in a conversation with K. P. S. Menon in February 1953—"How primitive it is to create a state on the basis of religion"—is also cited in support of the so-called Soviet bafflement at the creation of Pakistan.[10] However, Marx-

---

[10] See *The Evolution of Russia's Pakistan Policy*, a paper presented by Vijay Sen Budhraj at a seminar on socialism held under

ism gives reasonable explanation for the creation of Pakistan. Dyakov refers to the "peculiarities" of social development in certain areas of India, which were exploited by Muslim communal leaders and the British ruling circles, as the cause of its birth.

Later, Soviet scholars like Y. V. Gankovsky and L. R. Gordon Polonskaya developed this line of thinking in their work, A History of Pakistan (Moscow, 1946). They criticized the tendency among historians "to explain the formation of Pakistan by the intrigues of individual ill-wishers, and to deny the fact that the partition was prompted by the interests of certain classes and social groups" (p. 8). The Soviet writers posed a vital question: "How to explain ... that religion operated as a determinative factor in the political arrangement of India, a land that had always had a highly developed national liberation movement?" They answered it thus:

> The answer is to be found in the peculiar features of the development of the peoples of Northern and Central India, on the one hand, and in Britain's colonial policy, on the other....Many features in the formation of the Indian bourgeoisie helped the British in their designs. Trade and moneylending, the main source of primitive accumulation for the Indian bourgeoisie, were chiefly in Hindu hands [pp. 5-6].

It is significant to note, as Budhraj has rightly pointed out, that Soviet orientalists scrupulously avoided favouring the Congress or the League. They laid great emphasis on the harmful effect of disunity between the two major

---

the auspices of the Nehru Museum, New Delhi, 21 November 1969.

parties, which weakened the national liberation movement.

Pakistan's bid to assume leadership of pan-Islamic forces proved a stumbling-block for the improvement of relations with the Soviet Union.[11] Moscow condemned the convening of the first Islamic Economic Conference in Karachi. The growing pro-West orientation of Pakistan also made the Russians suspicious, and there were adverse comments in the Soviet press. V. V. Balabushevich referred to a secret agreement of Pakistan with Britain for military bases and speculated on the USA negotiating for similar facilities in the Northwest Frontier Province and elsewhere.[12] This fear was repeatedly voiced by Soviet writers as well as in the impressions of Soviet visitors to Pakistan in this period. Visits by Americans to Pakistan, particularly, to the northern areas close to the frontier of the Soviet Union, were obviously not liked. A Soviet visitor to Pakistan wrote:

At the end of 1949, four senators, accompanied by "all manners of experts" spent nearly a week in Pakistan. They went to Khyber Pass, studied the country around, made photographs of the locality. These activities indicated that the American and British imperialists are interested in Pakistan not only as a market and field of investment. They are out to make it one of their military bases.[13]

Pakistan's attitude in the Korean War also prevented the development of friendly ties with the USSR. In

[11] Sangat Singh, op. cit., p. 131.
[12] Trud, 21 November 1948.
[13] N. Gladkov, "In Pakistan—Travel Impressions," New Times, No. 21, 24 May 1950, p. 22.

London, Liaquat Ali Khan, publicly announced Pakistan's full support to the United Nations and denounced North Korea's action as a clear case of aggression. Pakistan offered a gift of 5,000 tons of wheat to the United Nations for use in South Korea. A Soviet weekly on international affairs described this "as Liaquat Ali Khan's servile zeal."[14]

Between 1950 and 1952 the Soviet press on several occasions voiced suspicions that Pakistan was moving close to the American camp to win the USA's support on Kashmir. *Izvestia* of 9 August 1950, carried a report about an assurance the American Ambassador had given Pakistan of support on Kashmir in return for Pakistan's participation in the Korean War. *Pravda* of 19 June 1952 quoted the Italian newspaper *Avanti* to suggest that if the Government of Pakistan became more amenable to collaboration with Washington, the USA was not only ready to offer Karachi economic and military assistance but its active support in the Kashmir dispute.

Dyakov, in his work published in 1952, was only expressing the general Soviet attitude when he wrote that Pakistan was used chiefly by Anglo-American imperialism for strengthening its influence in the Near and Middle East and that in the United Nations the Government of Pakistan "supports American policy much more openly than the Indian Government." Dyakov made a scathing criticism of Pan-Islamism and observed:

. . .in foreign policy the task of Pan-Islamism is to mask the Pakistan Government's reactionary policy of scraping together an anti-Soviet bloc among the Muslim countries of the Near and Middle East. By Pan-Islamic slogans and by demagogy about the common interests

[14] *New Times*, No. 28, 12 July 1950, pp. 19-20.

of all Muslims in the world, the Muslim League is trying to conceal the dependence of Pakistan's present policy on British and American *diktats* and to veil Pakistan's role as the bridgehead of the Anglo-American bloc. . . .[15]

Relations with India

The Soviet Union signed trade pacts with India in 1948, 1949, and 1951, agreeing to supply wheat in exchange for tea, tobacco, jute, and other primary products. Yet the volume of trade between the two countries remained insignificant.[16] In 1952, India was among the 42 countries which participated in the International Economic Conference held in Moscow. In his speech at the conference, the Chairman of the USSR Chamber of Commerce expressed his country's willingness to increase trade relations with India and other newly independent countries on mutually advantageous terms. He stated that trade could be balanced in terms of imports and exports and could be paid for in the currency of the country concerned.[17]

Indian traders who attended the conference were able to assess at first hand Soviet export and import potentialities. The Soviet Union's participation in the International Industrial Exhibition held in Bombay in 1952 gave Indians an opportunity to familiarize themselves with that country's industrial progress. The Soviet pavilion attracted a large crowd of visitors. Thus, despite failure to establish

[15] Cited in *Central Asian Review*, Vol. 5, No. 2, 1957, pp. 166-9.
[16] During 1953, Indo-Soviet trade amounted to Rs. 8.1 million both ways. (D. K. Rangnekar, "Economic Cooperation," *Seminar*, No. 73, September 1965.)
[17] *New Times*, No. 15, Supplement, 1952, pp. 6-7.

large-scale trade relations, a desire to increase economic relations with India had already become clear towards the end of Stalin's leadership. The report submitted to the XIX Congress of the CPSU in 1952 said the Soviet Union stood "for the development of trade and cooperation with other countries notwithstanding differences in social systems."[18]

Some recent Indian and Western publications on Indo-Soviet relations after independence have overstressed the rigid and critical early attitude of the Soviet Union to India and Pakistan. They conveniently ignore the friendly references which an impartial and unbiased reader is sure to find out for himself. To give some examples, the Zhdanov report to the Cominform in September 1947, from which critical references about India's "obedience and enslavement" to Anglo-American policies are profusely quoted, and which is cited in support of the negative Soviet attitude towards the new non-aligned states,[19] also said: "To the anti-imperialist camp are drawn Indonesia, Vietnam, India ...Egypt and Syria sympathise with it."[20]

Similarly, Dyakov who is liberally quoted to show the negative Soviet assessment of Gandhi, wrote an article on his death which began thus:

His name was inseparably associated with the Indian national liberation movement as it developed between World War I and last year's partition of India. Throughout this period Gandhi was the most influential of the leaders of the Indian National Congress. His

---

[18] New Times, No. 42, Supplement, 15 October 1952.
[19] J. A. Naik, Soviet Policy Towards India, Delhi, pp. 32-3.
[20] A. Zhdanov, "On The International Situation," Pravda, 22 October 1947.

influence extended far beyond the Congress, to the Indian population.

Unlike Indian political leaders of the earlier school, Gandhi was not afraid to draw the people into the political struggle. On the contrary, it was one of the features of his tactics to draw the great labouring masses into the movement. This could not but promote the political awakening of the people — the peasantry, the handicraftmen—and marked a definite stage in the process of drawing them into active political life. From this point of view, Gandhism played a certain progressive part.[21]

In the UN Security Council, the Soviet delegate paid a high tribute to Gandhi. He said:

On behalf of the delegation of the USSR to the United Nations, I should like, on the occasion of the tragic death of a great Indian, Mr Gandhi, to express our deepest sympathy with the Indian delegation, the Government of India and the whole Indian people.

As one of the most outstanding political leaders of India, Gandhi has undoubtedly left a deep imprint on the history of India and the Indian people. The name of Gandhi will always be associated with the struggle for national liberation which the Indian people have waged over so long a time.[22]

Soviet Union and the Kashmir Question

When tribesmen from the northwest frontier invaded Kashmir in October 1945 with the aid and connivance of

[21] New Times, 1948, No. 7, Feb. 11, 1948.
[22] Security Council Official Records, yr. 3, mtg. 238, p. 309.

Pakistan, the Soviet press fully exposed the imperialist machinations behind it. It noted that the preparations for aggression were made in the province which was ruled by a British Governor. "...British agents, holding out promises of easy plunder, incited the warlike Pathans to march on Kashmir as 'saviours' of Islam," wrote a Soviet journalist.[23] *Pravda* reported that the "Muslim army" which invaded Kashmir was organized by a British general.[24]

According to some writers, the Soviet Union took a "neutral," "non-committal" or "indifferent" attitude on Kashmir until Pakistan joined the Western military alliances, when it became pro-Indian in its own national interests.[25] But this is not true. The Soviet Union from the very beginning desired India and Pakistan to solve the question through their own efforts without any outside interference. It did not want to complicate the matter further by taking sides. The Western powers, on the other hand, favoured internationalization of the Kashmir question, seeking an opportunity to fish in troubled waters. It is now known from the account of A. Campbell-Johnsons, Lord Mountbatten's Press Secretary, that it was none other than the British Governor-General of India himself who devised a new strategem to embroil India in a protracted dispute with Pakistan in the UN. The plan to bring in the UN was finalized by Mountbatten's adviser, Lord Ismay.[26]

[23] *New Times*, No. 40, 1948, p. 25.

[24] *Pravda*, 3 November 1948.

[25] J. A. Naik, *op. cit.*, pp. 52-7; R. Vaidyanath, "Recent Trends in Soviet Policies Towards India and Pakistan," *International Studies*, Bombay, Vol. VII, No. 3, January 1966, p. 431; Arthur Stein, *India and the Soviet Union*, Chicago and London, 1969, pp. 27-8. Stein, however, admits that "the Soviets did not avail themselves of an opportunity to make political capital."

[26] Alan Campbell-Johnson, *Mission with Mountbatten*, London, 1961, pp. 250-1.

Campbell-Johnson recalls Mountbatten's Personal Secretary Ronnie (Captain S. Brockman) having told him that
"we have to get inside the problem or we will have no
influence at all."[27]

A Soviet journalist visiting Pakistan expressed his country's attitude on Kashmir by deploring Pakistan's allotment
of 50 per cent of its budget for military purposes. He
remarked that "the wrangling between the two dominions
impedes the economic and cultural progress of both."[28]
Regarding Kashmir, he wrote:

> The issue is more than two years old ... twice brought
> before the UN ... but there is no visible prospect of
> its being settled, as it is fanned surreptitiously by certain
> influential member states. For Britain, Kashmir is one
> of the means of keeping both dominions under her
> control.[29]

While avoiding any extreme action which might aggravate the already tangled question of Kashmir, A.
Gromyko, the Soviet delegate to the Security Council
showed sympathy for India's stand. Thus when the Indian
representative objected to the change in agenda from
"the situation in Jammu and Kashmir" to "the India-
Pakistan question," made under the influence of some
Western powers, Gromyko, supported him.[30] Again, when
in February 1948 the British and American delegates
opposed postponement of the Security Council discussion
to enable the Indian delegation to go home for consulta-

27 Ibid., p. 226.
28 New Times, No. 21, 24 May 1950, pp. 20-2.
29 Ibid.
30 SCOR, yr. 3, 1948, mtg. 231, p. 150.

tions, the representatives of Ukraine and the USSR supported the move for adjourning the Council till the Indian delegate returned.[31]   Even at this early period, as Campbell-
Johnson noted, the belief was spreading among the Indian
public "that India has most to hope from Soviet Russia."[32]

In 1952, the Soviet representative, Jacob Malik, outlined
in detail his country's view on Kashmir when the Security
Council took up the second report of the UN mediator,
Dr Graham, on Kashmir. Malik said, the main reason why
the Kashmir question had remained unsettled for four
years was that the Anglo-American powers had made proposals of an "annexationist, imperialist nature" to impose
their own solution on Kashmir.

> The purpose of these plans is interference by the
> United States and the United Kingdom in the internal
> affairs of Kashmir, prolongation of the dispute between
> India and Pakistan on the question...and the conver-
> sion of Kashmir into a protectorate of the United States
> and the United Kingdom under the pretext of rendering
> "assistance through the United Nations." Finally, the
> purpose of these plans ... is to secure the introduction
> of Anglo-American troops into the territory of Kashmir
> and convert it into their colony and a military strategic
> base.[33]

When the Security Council met again in December
1952, the Soviet delegate Valerin Zorin again reiterated
Moscow's strong opposition to induction of foreign troops
into Kashmir.

[31] SCOR, yr. 3, mtg. 245, pp. 129-30.
[32] Campbell-Johnson, op. cit., p. 286.
[33] Ibid., yr. 7., mtg. 570, pp. 13-4.

Indo-Soviet Cooperation in the United Nations

Even during this period when relations between the USSR and India were not particularly warm, there was considerable cooperation and mutual understanding between them in the United Nations, especially on questions relating to the admission of People's China and condemnation of the policy of apartheid pursued by South Africa.

Writing in *Pravda* on "The Situation in India," Dyakov expressed satisfaction that "the membership of the Indian delegation in the organisation of the United Nations has been changed and some progressive leaders have been included."[34] Earlier Foreign Minister Molotov had declared from the tribune of the Paris Peace Conference: "...the time is not far ... when India will enjoy happier days."

As early as September 1946 India raised the question of racial discrimination in South Africa in the UN General Assembly. The United States and Britain opposed India on the ground that it was an internal matter of South Africa and the UN had no jurisdiction over it. The Soviet delegate, however, supported the Indian proposal and opposed the suggestion of some Western powers that the question be settled through bilateral negotiations between the parties concerned, as no such negotiations, in his view, was likely to succeed.[35]

On another occasion, when the Indian delegate moved a resolution recommending that the international trust territories be administered with a view to speedily securing "self-government or independence under the collective

[34] *Pravda*, 21 October 1946.
[35] GAOR, Session 2, 1st Cttee., 110th and 112th Meetings, pp. 460-62 and 479-82.

guidance or supervision of the United Nations," the Soviet Union favoured it, whereas the USA and Britain opposed.[36]

In September 1950, India tabled a resolution in the First Committee of the General Assembly maintaining that the Government of the People's Republic of China was "the only government functioning in the Republic of China" and hence it should be granted representation in the General Assembly. A. Vyshinsky, the Soviet delegate, fully supported India.[37]

Soon after the start of the Korean War, Nehru sent a personal message to Stalin on 13 July 1950, saying that India aimed at localizing the conflict and desired to assist in a speedy peaceful settlement. He suggested that:

> Within the framework of the Council, or outside the Council through unofficial contact, the USSR, the United States, and China, with the assistance and co-operation of other peaceable states, could find a basis for the cessation of the conflict and for the final solution of the Korean problem.[38]

Nehru's peace initiative on Korea was very well received in the Soviet Union. It was prominently covered by all newspapers. *Pravda* continued to give the reaction of the world press to the Nehru-Stalin correspondence for six consecutive days. Stalin replied to Nehru's communication quite promptly, welcoming his initiative and suggesting that the Security Council should also hear the representative of the Korean people.[39] But the legalistic

[36] GAOR, 1947, 4th Cttee, mtg. 44, p. 92.
[37] GAOR, Session 5, plen. mtgs. 277 and 279.
[38] Keesing's Contemporary Archives, Vol. VIII, 1950-52, p. 10847.
[39] Ibid.

stand taken by the Indian delegate, Sir Benegal Narsing Rau, opposing participation by the North Korean representative in the deliberations of the Security Council, and India's failure to support the Soviet move to condemn the violation by the United States of China's air space in Manchuria and bombing of some of its villages, obstructed further cooperation between the two countries.[40]

When the armistice agreement was concluded, the General Assembly discussed the composition of the proposed political conference. Indian participation was opposed by the United States but supported by the Soviet Union.[41]

This survey of Soviet policies towards India and Pakistan shows that despite wide differences in outlook and policy some advance, although slow, towards mutual understanding and cooperation was surely made in this early period, at least in the case of India. By 1952 there were indications that the Soviet Union was poised to improve its relations with India. But relations with Pakistan were hamstrung as Soviet suspicions of its amenability to the cold-war designs of the Western Powers mounted. Already on a low key, they were to deteriorate further when Pakistan openly jumped onto the US bandwagon of military alliances.

---

[40] SCOR, yr. 5, mtgs. 494, No. 36, pp. 16-9 and 501, No. 43, pp 24-5.

[41] GAOR, Session 7, 1st Cttee, mtg. 623 and 625, 1952.

CHAPTER III

CLEARING SKY: TOWARDS NEW UNDERSTANDING, 1952-1955

AS INDIA DEMONSTRATED IN THE UN AND ELSEWHERE THAT its policy of non-alignment was truly independent and projected itself as a factor for peace in Korea and Indo-China, earlier Soviet mistrust of its intentions began to give way to a new understanding of its important role as a bridge between the East and the West in the cold war. By now the Soviet Union had consolidated its position; its defences had been strengthened with the acquisition of nuclear weapons and the war-shattered economy had been reconstructed to such an extent that it could think of meaningful economic cooperation with newly independent states like India and Pakistan.

Stalin was only giving expression to the changed situation in the USSR when in reply to a question by American newspapers editors he said: "The peaceful coexistence of capitalism and communism is fully possible...."[1] One of Stalin's last theoretical statements, *Economic Problems of Socialism in the USSR* (2 October 1952), also hinted

---

[1] Denise Folliot, ed., *Documents on International Affairs, 1952*, London, 1955, p. 225.

at the possibilities of economic cooperation between the socialist and the capitalist countries. This idea was re-affirmed in Malenkov's report to the 19th Party Congress held in the same year.

Stalin met S. Radhakrishnan—when he was Indian Ambassador in Moscow—twice. At their second meeting in April 1952 he assured Radhakrishnan that all major East-West problems could be resolved peacefully.[2] K. P. S. Menon, who replaced Radhakrishnan as ambassador late in 1952, was among the last foreigners to see Stalin alive, only a fortnight before his death. At the meeting with Menon on 17 February 1953, Stalin showed interest in Indo-Pakistani relations and commended the formation of a federation of the two countries as an "ideal solution" of their many problems. He expressed his appreciation for India's policy of secularism, which he called "just the right one."[3] An air of change could thus be felt during the last days of Stalin.

Stalin's successors continued to lend support to this new course. Malenkov publicly praised India's contribution to the efforts of peace-loving countries. In his address to the Supreme Soviet on 8 August 1953 he said:

Our relations with India are becoming stronger and our cultural ties are growing. We hope that in the future relations between India and the USSR will grow stronger and develop in a spirit of friendly cooperation.[4]

But the Soviet Premier in his statement also said that

[2] See Times of India, 5 March 1953, and Hindustan Times, 22 November 1965.

[3] K. P. S. Menon, The Flying Troika, London, 1963, pp. 29-30.

[4] Pravda, 9 August 1953.

the Soviet Union "attaches great importance to the successful development of relations with Pakistan and to strengthening every kind of relations between the two states."[5] This reference to Pakistan along with India was significant. The Soviet Union has always desired to have friendly relations with both the states in the subcontinent. She had not given up hopes of a favourable response from Pakistan in spite of rumours of an impending military alliance with the United States.

The Soviet attitude towards Pakistan naturally grew critical as the latter gravitated more and more towards a military alliance with the USA. Nehru's severe criticism of American military aid to Pakistan in 1953 was given wide publicity in the Soviet press. *Pravda* criticized Washington's designs to establish military bases in Pakistan and held it responsible for deterioration in India's relations with the USA.[6] Earlier, another article in the same paper pointed out the adverse effect of the American move on India's efforts to improve relations with its neighbour:

The Indian people cannot but be alarmed seeing the attempts to set up an aggressive bloc right on India's borders, which will invariably lead to the building of foreign bases and airfields on the territories of India's neighbour and to militarisation of the countries with which it is attempting to maintain closer relations.[7]

[5] *Ibid.*
[6] *Pravda*, 3 December 1953.
[7] *Pravda*, 27 September 1953. Earlier in August, the paper had expressed the hope that the Kashmir question would be solved through bilateral negotiations between the leaders of the two countries. It praised efforts of the Indian and Pakistani Prime Ministers to solve this problem by peaceful means (*Pravda*, 22 August 1953).

Again a *Pravda* columnist accused the USA of trying to use its negotiations with Pakistan to exert political pressure on India, which "refused to submit to American dictation."[8] *Pravda* published as many as 16 articles and news items on Indian reactions to American bases in Pakistan.[9] On 30 November 1953, the Soviet Ambassador called on the Pakistani Foreign Secretary and delivered a strong note which drew the Pakistan Government's attention to the fact that the Soviet Government could not be indifferent to reports about Pakistan joining the Middle East Treaty Organisation as such a development would have "a direct bearing on the security of the Soviet Union."[10]

In 1954, Soviet-Pak relations were at a low ebb, because Pakistan had become a member of the US military alliances. Yet normal contacts continued in some fields. In January 1954, preliminary trade talks were held as scheduled for a trade agreement. The Soviet Union also offered technical assistance to Pakistan. In October, four Pakistani officials and three businessmen set out on a one-month study tour of the Soviet Union. The Soviet Red Cross Society sent Rs 50,000 to help flood sufferers in Pakistan in September 1954. Two Soviet groups, including a cultural delegation, visited Pakistan the same year. Pakistan's co-sponsorship of the Bandung Conference was also welcomed in the Soviet press.

The Soviet Union worked for representation of India on all international forums on disarmament. In 1954, it proposed an enlargement of the UN Disarmament Sub-

8 *Pravda*, 21 December 1953.
9 J. A. Naik, *op. cit.*, p. 71.
10 *Pravda*, 2 December 1953.

Commission and the inclusion of India, Czechoslovakia, and the People's Republic of China. The Soviet delegate Vyshinsky had a dig at British representative, Sir Pierson Dixon, for opposing India: "After all, India is a member of the Commonwealth. . . . Why do you object to a member of your own family?"[11]   Moscow hailed Nehru's proposal for the prohibition of nuclear weapons as a substantial step towards disarmament. His statement against the US system of military alliances was given wide coverage in the Soviet press.

At the Geneva Conference of 1954 on Indo-China, India's representative Krishna Menon played an important role in the backstage negotiations. Molotov received Menon several times and gave a reception in his honour. Molotov proposed India's name for a neutral nations' commission to supervise the ceasefire in Indo-China.[12] At Geneva Molotov spoke thus about India's place in international affairs.

Who can deny that a country like India, with a population of more than 300 million people, has entered into a new historic arena? Not long ago India was a colonial country. But now nobody can deny that India is occupying a very important place among the countries which are consolidating their national independence and striving to secure its weighty place in world affairs.[13]

In July 1953, the USSR gave 4 million roubles to the UN Expanded Programme of Technical Assistance for projects in underdeveloped areas. At a meeting of the

11 *Hindu,* 20 April 1954.
12 *New Times,* No. 24, 1954, Supplement, pp. 14-21.
13 *Pravda,* 30 April 1954.

Economic Commission for Asia and the Far East in February 1954, the Soviet spokesman expressed willingness to provide aid to Asian nations with "no political strings attached." The prospect of such aid was attractive to India because the Soviet Union was only too willing to help the expansion of India's public sector, particularly in heavy industry. Negotiations for Soviet assistance in building a steel plant began in September 1954. An agreement was signed for a plant at Bhilai, in Madhya Pradesh, in February 1955.

Cultural contacts between India and the Soviet Union began to increase on an unprecedented scale. Rajkumari Amrit Kaur visited Moscow in June 1953 at the invitation of the Soviet Government. On her return she spoke of the Soviet people's desire for friendly relations with India and their ardent desire for peace.[14] The following month Indira Gandhi travelled extensively in the USSR for nearly two months. She too testified to the warm feelings of friendship towards India everywhere.[15] The same month a delegation of Indian women visiting the USSR received a warm welcome.[16] Within a year and a half after Stalin's death as many as 14 Indian delegations, from a football team and film artists to industrialists, visited Moscow.[17] The frequency of these contacts rose considerably in August-September 1954 and remained high thereafter. In those two months delegations of Indian teachers and students, scientists, farmers, industrialists, and artists visited the USSR. On 3 August, the two countries announced an exchange of military attaches to their respec-

---

[14] *Pravda*, 22 June 1953.
[15] *Pravda*, 30 August 1953.
[16] *Pravda*, 12 July 1953.
[17] J. A. Naik, *op. cit.*, p. 70.

tive embassies.[18] From 24 to 29 September five Indian films were shown in 19 Soviet cities. In Moscow alone 1 million people saw these films. Among the films shown were Raj Kapoor's *Awara* and Bimal Roy's *Do Bigha Zamin*. In December 1953, the Soviet Deputy Health Minister paid a return visit to India. A delegation of Soviet artists led by the Deputy Minister of Culture came to India in January 1954 and a delegation of the USSR Academy of Sciences also toured India.

In 1954 India took the initiative with China in expounding Panchsheel, the Five Principles of peaceful coexistence which formed part of the preamble to the India-China Agreement on Tibet. The principles received attention and applause from the Soviet Union. A *Pravda* editorial commending these principles said:

There cannot be any doubt that the acceptance of these important principles by the Asian as well as other countries would diminish the possibility of wars, serve to alleviate tension in world community and improve the valuable cooperation between countries.[19]

On the anniversary of the October Revolution in 1954, the Central Committee of the Communist Party of the Soviet Union issued a slogan for India which said: "May the friendship and cooperation between the people of India and the Soviet Union widen and strengthen for the protection of peace in the whole world." In an editorial *Pravda* acknowledged India's "valuable contribution for strengthening peace."[20] In 1955, high Soviet state and

[18] Arthur Stein, *op. cit.*, p. 211.
[19] *Pravda,* 1 July 1954.
[20] *Pravda,* 28 October 1954.

party dignitaries attended the Republic Day reception at the Indian Embassay in Moscow with a large number of artists, writers, and public figures.[21] *Pravda* in a long article noted:

> The Soviet people are confident that relations between India and the Soviet Union will strengthen and grow in an atmosphere of friendship and cooperation. On this day of the fifth anniversary of the Republic of India the Soviet people express their feelings of high sympathy to the great Indian people for consolidating their independence, for peace in Asia and in the whole world.[22]

In February 1955, the Supreme Soviet adopted a declaration recommending the adoption by the rest of the world of the Five Principles on which China and India based their relations with other countries.[23] By now the Soviet leadership had undergone a change, Bulganin having replaced Malenkov. But this made no difference to the growing warmth of friendship with India. In a report to the Supreme Soviet, Molotov referred to the increasing recognition of India in world affairs:

> It is a fact of great historic importance that colonial India is no more, and there is an Indian Republic instead. This important transformation is characteristic of postwar development in Asia. India's international prestige as a new and important factor of peace and friendship among nations is increasing.[24]

21 *Pravda*, 27 January 1955.
22 *Pravda*, 26 January 1955.
23 *Pravda*, 10 February 1955.
24 *New Times*, No. 7, Supplement, 1955, p. 13.

The sky of Indo-Soviet relations had cleared up by February 1955 and the bright sun of friendship began to rise. A new understanding had been reached between the two countries for their future cooperation for peace and prosperity. With Pakistan, the relations of the Soviet Union still lacked the warmth and understanding which characterized its relations with India. The intrusion of the USA into the affairs of the subcontinent by drawing Pakistan into the orbit of its military pacts, marred the prospects of an Indo-Pakistan *detente* and led Pakistan to drift away from her northern neighbour.

CHAPTER IV

FRIENDSHIP THROUGH TRIALS AND TRIBULATIONS, 1955-1965

JAWAHARLAL NEHRU'S SECOND VISIT TO THE USSR,[1] AND HIS first as Prime Minister of India, in June 1955, opened a new chapter in the friendly relations between the people of India and the Soviet Union. This was followed by the historic return visit of Khrushchev and Bulganin, in November 1955. Incidentally, it was the first time the Soviet leaders had visited a non-Communist country. This exchange of state visits affirmed the tremendous goodwill that had been generated in the preceding two years in relations between the two countries. Taken together, these visits ushered in the era of warm Indo-Soviet relations.

A marked improvement in the international climate—signing of the treaty of Austrian neutrality by the Big Four, restoration of friendly relations between the Soviet Union and Yugoslavia, new Soviet overtures to West Germany for establishing normal diplomatic, trade and cultural rela-

[1] Nehru went to the Soviet Union for the first time in 1927 with his father Motilal Nehru.

tions, and the Bandung Conference of Afro-Asian countries —formed the historic backdrop of Nehru's visit to the Soviet Union. It was preceded by a large Indian parliamentary delegation in May.[2] The Soviet authorities had made great preparations for Nehru's visit. Extracts from his writings and speeches and writeups on his life and activities figured in the Soviet press prominently in the week before his arrival. Copies of the Russian edition of *Discovery of India* were sold out in no time in several leading cities. *Pravda* wrote an editorial welcoming his visit and said:

Today the Prime Minister of India is visiting our country. From the bottom of their hearts the Soviet people welcome the growing friendship with the people of India and say: Long live this friendship!

The paper dwelt on the historical ties between the Indian and Soviet people at some length, mentioning Afanasi Nikitin and Rabindranath Tagore, and stressed that the two nations always had friendly relations and high mutual respect.

Nehru, who was accompanied by Indira Gandhi, was greeted warmly everywhere on his extensive tour of the various Soviet Republics. One distinguishing feature of the tour was that he not only met high state and party officials but also addressed the public. He was the first head of a non-communist state to address large audiences in Moscow, Leningrad, Kiev, Tashkent, Alma Ata, Samarkand, Ashkhabad, Sverdlovsk, and other cities. Nehru wound up his whirlwind tour with a big public meeting, attended by 80,000 to 100,000 people, in Moscow's

[2] *Hindu*, 30 May, 1955

Dynamo Stadium. This huge public rally, affirming Indo-Soviet friendship, was attended by Khrushchev and Bulganin and other top Soviet leaders.

The joint communique issued at the end of the visit reaffirmed the faith of both countries in *Panchsheel* and expressed their desire for promoting further cultural and economic cooperation between the two countries. It asserted that the Five Principles of peaceful coexistence were "capable of wider application and that in the observance of these principles by nations . . . lies the main hope of banishing fear and mistrust from their minds and thus of lowering world tensions."[3] The fear of the big powers by smaller and weaker states was recognized by the two Prime Ministers, who felt that it was essential "to dispel this fear in all possible ways." The remedy suggested by them was "to adhere unflinchingly to the principles of peaceful coexistence."

They stressed that there was ample scope within the framework of the principles for the development of cultural economic and technical cooperation between the two states and maintained:

> The fact that each country is following a system which is moulded by its own genius, traditions and environment should be no bar to such cooperation. Indeed, the essence of true coexistence, in which both Prime Ministers have profound faith, is that states of different social structures can exist side by side in peace and concord and work for the common good.[4]

Nehru's visit produced a powerful impression on the Soviet leaders, who made several references to its signific-

---

[3] *New Times*, No. 28, Supplement, 1955.
[4] *Ibid*.

ance in their subsequent meetings with heads of other states. Thus, when the Big Four met at Geneva, Bulganin mentioned Nehru's visit as an event of great importance.[5] The joint-communique issued when Ho Chi Minh visited the USSR praised India's role in enunciating the Five Principles.[6] In his report to the Supreme Soviet on the Geneva Conference of the Big Four in 1955, Bulganin again referred to Nehru's visit and noted that both countries "take the same position on urgent problems concerning the struggle for peace, and this is of great importance in the settlement of pressing Asian and Far Eastern problems and in easing international tension."[7] In June 1955, in his speech at the tenth anniversary session of the United Nations, Molotov referred to the visit of Nehru as "especially noteworthy" for lessening international tension and promoting peace.[8]

The Soviet trip made a tremendous impact on Nehru, who expressed his gratitude to his hosts by saying, "I am leaving my heart behind."[9] From Moscow, Nehru went to other European countries before returning to India. In Dusseldorf he reminded his West German hosts of the Soviet fear of a rearmed Germany. It was necessary, he advised, to consider the apprehensions of the Soviet Union, which felt itself to be encircled by hostile bases. In Belgrade, Nehru spoke against the use of the term "iron curtain,"[10] remarking that the greatest iron curtain was the one in people's minds, which, like a wall, prevented them from looking at the world as it was.

[5] New Times, No. 30, 1955, p. 15.
[6] New Times, No. 30, Supplement, 1955.
[7] Pravda, 5 August 1955.
[8] New Times, No. 27, 1955, Supplement.
[9] Hindu, 12 July 1955.
[10] Cited by Arthur Stein, op. cit., p. 69.

The Western press did not take kindly to Nehru's visit to the USSR. The *New York Times* warned Nehru that he might be "skilfully mousetrapped" in Moscow.[11] The *London Times* commented editorially on June 24 that the Indo-Soviet communique would contribute little to the "peace and equanimity of the world. One cannot doubt that it is his [Nehru's] desire to contribute to world peace.... But it is a pity that Mr Nehru's contribution to this ideal should have been a general acceptance of the Soviet policies."

Soviet leaders also availed themselves of the opportunity to express their warm feelings of friendship towards India at the opening in Moscow in October 1955 of exhibitions of Indian art and culture and handicrafts. *Pravda* carried a special article on the exhibits of Indian art and culture, describing them as "a clear and striking example of the talent and love of work of the Indian people."[12] One of the slogans on the anniversary of the October Revolution said: "Greetings to the great Indian people."[13]

On 18 November 1955, Khrushchev and Bulganin and several other high officials arrived in Delhi on a state visit. The Soviet guests stayed in India three weeks and visited many places in different parts of the country. Their travels extended from New Delhi to Chandigarh, Jaipur, Poona, Bombay, Bangalore, Madras, Coimbatore, Calcutta, Srinagar, and various other places. In all they visited 11 states and received a tumultuous welcome everywhere. The spontaneous and mammoth public receptions convinced the Soviet leaders of the great depth of Indian people's feelings towards the Soviet Union. They extended their

---

11 *New York Times*, 11 June 1955.
12 *Pravda*, 9 October 1955.
13 *Pravda*, 25 October 1955.

country's wholehearted support to India against Western colonialism, and at Calcutta Khrushchev expressed the hope that "sooner or later ... Goa will free itself from foreign rule and will become an integral part of the Republic of India."

The visiting leaders gave their unqualified support to India on Kashmir. On 10 December at a public reception in Srinagar, Khrushchev said that the Kashmir problem, created by some colonial powers, had been solved by the people of Kashmir with their decision to join the Indian Republic and the Soviet Government accepted this position. Khrushchev condemned the partition of India on religious grounds. He said:

> In the Soviet Union we have found good solutions to both the questions of nationalities and the question of the freedom of conscience. Every citizen in our country can order his religious life in the way he considers necessary.
>
> I am saying this in order to make our position on this question clearer to you....
>
> One can therefore say that it was not the difference in religious faiths of the people which was the principal factor in the creation of Pakistan and in its separation from the one united state of India. Some states which have for a long time followed the well-known principle of "divide and rule" actively helped in this.
>
> We are absolutely convinced that when passions have calmed down and the people realise the significance of such an artificial division of India, they will regret it.[14]

This statement did not imply hostility towards Pakistan.

[14] *Pravda* and *Izvestia*, 11 December 1955.

When Khrushchev declared that "the question of Kashmir as one of the states of the Republic of India has been settled by the people of Kashmir themselves," he added that "both sides must show a greater desire to maintain peace in this region since the development of both India and Pakistan can only take place under conditions of peaceful coexistence."[15]

Later, in his report to the Supreme Soviet on his Asian trip, Khrushchev spelt out the Soviet objectives of developing friendly relations with India in very clear terms. He expected friendship with India to help the USSR improve its relations with other states. He said:

> ...We do not want to be limited to friendly relations with one, two or a few states. We want to be friends with all states.
>
> We are, therefore, glad when our friends develop friendly relations with other states, including those states with which for some reason or another we may have strained and cold relations. Through our friend, for that is what we consider India, we hope to improve our relations with these states.[16]

Referring to Pakistan's membership of the Baghdad Pact, Khrushchev said: "After all, it is a fact that Pakistan's relations with India, Afghanistan and the Soviet Union leave much to be desired."[17] He also told the Supreme Soviet that India was a neutral state and "deserved trust and respect from us as well from other states," and "if Pakistan were to adopt the same independent attitude...

15 Ibid.
16 Pravda and Izvestia, 30 December. 1955.
17 Ibid.

conditions would be provided for the establishment of friendly relations between Pakistan and neighbouring countries."[18]

Both the Soviet and Indian leaders made it quite plain that they desired to strengthen friendly relations between their countries without in any way prejudicing the development of their relations with other countries. Khrushchev told the Supreme Soviet:

Both we and our Indian friends would like to develop and strengthen our friendly relations in a way which would not change the friendly relations of India or of the Soviet Union with other states.[19]

During their visit the Soviet leaders expressed their admiration for Gandhi's leadership. Bulganin said in Bombay:

You had an outstanding leader who did much for your country . . . we have a proper respect for his memory. . . . We, the pupils of Lenin, do not share the philosophical views of Gandhi, but consider him an outstanding leader who contributed much to the development of your people's peace-loving views and their struggle for independence.[20]

[18] Ibid.

[19] Ibid. Earlier during his visit to the USSR, Nehru had also spoken in similar vein: "Let our coming together be because we like each other and we wish to cooperate and not because we dislike others or wish to do them injury" (Jawaharlal Nehru's Speeches, 1953-57, New Delhi, 1959, pp. 304-5). Sisir Gupta thinks that these statements of Indian and Soviet leaders evolved "a more stable basis of Indo-Soviet relations." See his article, "India and the Soviet Union," Current History, March 1963.

[20] Pravda, 20 November 1955.

Towards the end of the tour a joint communique on economic relations was issued, in which both governments agreed to exchange trade representatives to look after their growing trade. The Soviet Union agreed to supply machinery and necessary help for oil exploration and construction of hydroelectric projects in India.[21] Khrushchev told a meeting of the Parliamentary Association for the Promotion of Hindi that on their return they would do everything necessary to "enable the Soviet people to have more opportunities for studying Indian languages, Hindi in the first place."

As a follow-up of their tour, Anastas Mikoyan, First Vice-Premier, arrived in India in March 1956 to work out details for Indo-Soviet trade. By 1955 the volume of Indo-Soviet trade had surpassed the level set by the 1953 agreement. After the visit of the Soviet leaders an added warmth could be noticed in relations between the two countries in all spheres. Top Soviet party and state leaders attended the Republic Day reception at the Indian Embassy in Moscow on 26 January 1956. Soviet magazines and journals wrote very appreciative articles on India. V. Avarin titled his article, published in *International Affairs*, "India—a Great Power."[22] The famous Soviet orientalist, E. Zhukov, wrote on Gandhi's role in history and admitted that many Soviet orientalists, including himself, had an "incorrect assessment of his activities" in the past. Zhukov declared that "despite certain defects Gandhism was a genuinely popular anti-imperialist movement."[23] In June 1956, when the Vice-President Radhakrishnan visited Moscow, the first volume of his work, *Indian Philosophy,*

[21] *Pravda*, 14 December 1955.
[22] *International Affairs*, Moscow, February 1956.
[23] *New Times*, No. 6, 1956.

was published in Russian and he was made an honorary professor of Moscow University.

The 20th Party Congress of the CPSU vindicated Nehru's belief in a strong trend within the USSR towards restoration of healthy socialist democracy. On 20 March he told the Indian Parliament that "there can be no doubt that the CPSU Congress has developed a new line and a new policy." He called it "a step towards the creation of conditions favourable to the pursuit of a policy of peaceful coexistence...important for us as well as others."[24] Nehru firmly believed that internal reforms in the USSR would contribute to an easing of international tensions. It was due to his efforts that the Commonwealth Prime Ministers' Conference in July 1956 adopted a joint statement which indicated the participants willingness to facilitate increased contacts with the USSR.[25] Increasingly cordial cooperative relations with the USSR had by now become the cornerstone of India's foreign policy.

The Suez crisis revealed the common approach of India and the Soviet Union towards predatory character of Western colonialism. Nehru's reaction to the Anglo-French-Israeli invasion of Egypt in October 1956 was prompt and sharp. The Soviet Union also sharply reacted to the Western powers' attack on Egypt, condemning the aggressive action of Israel, Britain, and France and warning them of "the dangerous consequences." At the London conference on the Suez Canal the Soviet Union supported the proposals made by the Indian delegation. Soviet Foreign Minister Shepilov termed the Indian proposals "a plan for a just and peaceful settlement of the Suez problem."[26]

[24] Lok Sabha Debates, Vol. 2, No. 27, Cols. 304-48.
[25] Cited by Arthur Stein, op. cit., p. 83.
[26] New Times, No. 36, Supplement, 1956, pp. 36-7.

About the same time events in Hungary put a severe strain on the rapidly growing Indo-Soviet understanding. Speaking in Parliament, Nehru described these events as "tragic" but showed his inclination to accept the Yugoslav assessment of the situation in Hungary, which described it as a revolt inspired by internal reactionaries with foreign instigation and aid.[27] India abstained from voting on the resolution the UN General Assembly passed on 4 November which condemned the Soviet "intervention" and instructed the Secretary-General to set up a committee to investigate conditions in Hungary. India found the tone and content of the resolution objectionable. It also abstained on the 9 November Resolution of the General Assembly calling for the withdrawal of Soviet troops and the subsequent holding of elections in Hungary under the auspices of the UN.[28]

On 4 December, Nehru told the Rajya Sabha that the process of liberalization and democratization might have been completed peacefully in Hungary, as in Poland, if the Hungarian leadership had handled the situation prudently. He associated the Soviet action in Budapest with the Suez question: "I imagine that in Hungary they would have escaped that danger also if exactly at that time the Anglo-French invasion had not come in."[29]

Nehru's main concern in the case of Hungary centred on localizing the conflict and alleviating the people's suf-

[27] Lok Sabha Debates, pt. 2, vol. 9, No. 3 (20 November 1956), Col. 381.

[28] Later, when the General Assembly was discussing the Anglo-French-Israeli attack on Egypt, the Indian delegate, Krishna Menon, voiced criticism of the Soviet Government's Hungarian policy. But his tone differed radically from the Western criticism of the Soviet action.

[29] Rajya Sabha Official Record, Vol. 15, No. 12 (4 December 1956), Col. 1534.

fering. He strongly supported UN food and medical shipments and other relief measures. The Indian delegation, with those of Ceylon and Indonesia, moved a resolution which, while incorporating the Western charges against the Soviet Union and the Soviet denial of them, urged the Hungarian Government "to permit observers designated by the Secretary-General to enter the territory of Hungary, to travel freely therein, and to report their finding to the Secretary-General."

The Soviet delegate voted against this resolution, but showed great consideration for its sponsors. He preferred to base his opposition to it on the ground that it was not acceptable to the Hungarian Government, which considered it interference with its domestic affairs.[30] The fact that the two states, while differing with each other on certain important international issues, could yet continue to show mutual regard and respect only testified to the maturity of the friendly understanding between them. Despite strong criticism from certain sections in the country, the Government of India persistently refused to take an anti-Soviet attitude on Hungary and did not allow it to mar the smooth course of friendship with the USSR.

The Soviet policy of pleading for the inclusion of India in big power discussions of vital Asian questions and disarmament found added support in the post-1955 period. In the Middle East crisis of July 1958, which arose as a result of the landing of British and American troops in Jordan and Lebanon following the revolution in Iraq, Khrushchev sent messages to the heads of the US, British, French, and Indian Governments on 19 July proposing that they meet with the the head of the Soviet Govern-

[30]GAOR, Session 11, plen. mtgs., Vol. 1, 1956-57, mtg., 587, p. 188.

ment immediately and take measures to end the military conflict. Nehru welcomed the Soviet initiative and informed that if the proposed conference took place he would gladly participate. When the Western leaders rejected this summit proposal and suggested that the Security council should deal with the question, Khrushchev insisted that India be invited to the Council meeting.[31] Britain and France, however, opposed India's participation.

The Soviet Union also sought to associate India with a summit conference of the Big Four on disarmament which it proposed in late 1958. It was largely on the initiative of the Soviet Union that the 10-member Disarmament Committee appointed by the UN General Assembly was enlarged to include eight neutral countries, including India. In 1962, the Soviet Premier proposed that the 18-Nation Disarmament Committee meet in March and that the heads of government personally attend its first sesson. In a letter to Nehru he wrote:

I can say, as I expressed on many occasions and personally to you when we met, that the Soviet Government views highly the contribution of the Government of India in strengthening the force of peace-loving governments and people and helping the realisation of this great object in life. Your stand, Mr. Nehru, in supporting the general and complete disarmament ... has always been receiving understanding and respect in our country.[32]

An achievement of the 18-Nation Disarmament Com-

[31] Pravda, 24 July 1958.
[32] Pravda, 4 March 1962.

mittee was drawing up the Test Ban Treaty. India led the list of signatories to the treaty in Moscow.

When Nehru formed a new government after the general election in 1957, the Soviet leaders sent greetings to him. In his message the Soviet Premier said:

> Mankind cannot evaluate the great contribution of India and yourself in the big task of preserving and strengthening peace. We are confident that the government headed by you will in future, too, steadfastly champion the cause of peace and international cooperation.
>
> The Soviet people greatly value the brotherly friendship with the Indian people, for the growth of which you did so much and which is already demonstrating its firmness as a factor in the world.[33]

In his policy report to the Supreme Soviet, Shepilov also referred to Nehru's foreign policy as "a striking example of a genuine peace policy." Shepilov also expressed his government's desire to establish friendly relations with Pakistan.[34] When the Bhilai steel plant was officially commissioned in February 1959 *Pravda* carried a long article on Indo-Soviet friendship, and when the plant's second furnace was commissioned towards the end of 1959 Khrushchev personally sent a message to Nehru expressing his hope that "the future Soviet-Indian economic and technical cooperation, which was born at Bhilai, would grow on all sides."[35] When India's Third Five-Year Plan was facing an acute shortage of foreign exchange the Soviet Government sent a delegation of experts in February 1959 and offered a fresh

[33] *Pravda*, 4 May 1957.
[34] *New Times*, No. 8, Supplement, 1957.
[35] *Pravda*, 30 December 1959.

credit of 1,500 million roubles. In August 1960, it offered a further credit of 500 million roubles.

As in the past, exchange of state visits with high Soviet dignitaries continued in 1960. In January 1960, Soviet President Voroshilov visited India, and in February Khrushchev paid his second visit. On this visit the Soviet leader addressed a joint session of Parliament, had talks with Indian leaders, went to the Bhilai steel plant and the Suratgarh state farm in Rajasthan for which the Soviet Union had gifted equipment. He was given civic receptions at Delhi and Calcutta.

The Soviet and the Sino-Indian Conflict

In mid-1959 several skirmishes took place between Indian and Chinese patrols along the Himalayan border which brought to the world's attention the existence of a dispute between Asia's two larger nations. The first official Soviet comment appeared in the Tass bulletin of 9 September and called these incidents "deplorable." The statement said:

... The Chinese and Soviet peoples are linked by the unbreakable bonds of fraternal friendship.... Friendly cooperation between the USSR and India is successfully developing in keeping with the idea of peaceful coexistence.... Its [the dispute's] inspirers are trying to discredit the idea of peaceful coexistence between states with different social systems and to prevent the strengthening of the Asian people's solidarity in the struggle for consolidation of national independence.[36]

[36] Pravda, 10 September 1959.

Although sceptics in India drew pointed attention to the phrases "fraternal friendship" with China and "friendly cooperation" with India and inferred that the Soviet Union leaned towards China, a student of international affairs can testify today with the benefit of hindsight that the Tass statement was aimed at the Chinese splitters of Asian unity and their denigration of the concept of peaceful coexistence.

Four years later, the Chinese themselves let the cat out of the bag when an article in the *Peking Review* of 8 November 1963, entitled "The Truth How the Leaders of the CPSU Have Allied Themselves With India Against China" criticized the publication of the Tass statement of 9 September despite Peking's objections.

Nehru, who had a deep insight into the background of the Sino-Soviet ideological dispute, which had been simmering since 1956, correctly described the Tass statement as "a fair one and an unusual one for the Soviet Government to sponsor."

On 30 October in a major policy speech before the Supreme Soviet, the Soviet Premier referred to the incident in these words:

> We are especially sorry that these incidents have resulted in loss of life to both sides. Nothing can make up for the loss of the parents and relatives of the victims. We would be happy if there were no more incidents on the Sino-Indian frontier, if the existing frontier disputes were settled by way of friendly negotiations to the mutual satisfaction of both sides.[37]

The reaction in official circles in New Delhi was that the Soviet attitude indirectly favoured India. Though the

[37] *Pravda*, 1 November 1959.

Soviets had not expressed themselves on the merits of the dispute, they had not supported the Chinese.

The visit of President Rajendra Prasad to the USSR in June 1960 once again manifested the warm feelings towards India. Brezhnev said in his welcome speech:

> Warm friendship and wide cooperation between our governments and peoples is very bright evidence of the fact that nothing can stop the irresistible longings of the progressive forces from establishing new relations based on principles of peaceful coexistence between countries.[38]

At the 1960 session of the UN General Assembly, Khrushchev, who was indignant over the Congo muddle, which in his opinion resulted from the inability of the UN Secretary-General to withstand Western pressure, suggested that the post be abolished and a "troika," an executive agency representing the West, the Socialist camp and the neutral nations, be created instead. Later, when Patrice Lumumba was murdered, the Soviet Prime Minister sent a message to Nehru reiterating his earlier demand for Hammarskjoeld's replacement. Lack of response from India's side, however, did not impair Moscow's relations with New Delhi.

In September 1961, Nehru paid a four-day visit to Moscow on his return from Belgrade, where he had gone to attend the conference of non-aligned countries. With Kwame Nkrumah of Ghana he carried a message from the conference to the heads of government of the USSR and the USA to stop nuclear tests and resume negotiations

[38] *Pravda,* 21 June 1960.

on disarmament. At a public meeting in Moscow, Nehru mentioned this message. In his reply Khrushchev defended the Soviet resumption of tests on the ground that the Western powers were following an aggressive line by refusing to sign a German peace treaty, had built aggressive military blocs around the Soviet Union and had not responded to the Soviet proposals for complete and total disarmament. This had compelled the Soviet Union to step up its defence preparations, the Soviet leader explained.[39]

In the joint communique issued at the end of the visit the Indian Prime Minister agreed with his Soviet counterpart that "the fact of the existence of the German states at present could not be ignored and that any attempt to change the frontiers will have dangerous consequences." As noted earlier, Nehru had spoken after his 1955 visit of "the fear of a rearmed Germany which existed in Eastern Europe."[40]

Goa and Kashmir

Soviet support to India's claim on Goa, like its support to any issue relating to the liquidation of colonialism in general, had been made public from the very beginning. On their 1955 visit to India the Soviet leaders had hoped that Goa would soon become a part of India. When the Indian forces liberated Goa from the colonial Portuguese yoke, Pravda flashed the news: "Portuguese colonialists

[39] Pravda, 9 September 1961.
[40] J. A. Naik's attempt to attribute the reference to the German states in the joint communique to Soviet pressure on India to obtain a quid pro quo for the first Soviet veto on Kashmir is highly speculative (op. cit., pp. 123-4).

are ousted from India! Indian forces liberate Goa, Daman and Diu."[41] When the Indian forces marched into Goa, President Brezhnev was in Bombay. He supported the Indian Government's action in a speech.

The Soviet Prime Minister sent a message to Nehru expressing his government's full support to India. He hailed the liberation of Goa as "a great contribution to the noble task of the people's struggle for the complete and urgent liquidation of the shameful colonial system."[42] He termed it "a completely lawful and rightful act." When the Western powers brought forward a resolution in the Security Council to censure India the Soviet Union blocked it with a prompt veto.

The Kashmir issue figured again in the Council in early 1957 when Pakistan raised it on the ground that India was integrating the state as a constituent part of the Indian Republic from 26 January 1957. On 14 February, Britain and the USA cosponsored a resolution on Kashmir. The resolution noted that "demilitarisation preparatory to the holding of a free and impartial plebiscite under UN auspices has not been achieved in accordance with the resolutions of the UN Commission for India and Pakistan." It called for "the use of a temporary UN force in connection with demilitarisation" and authorized the Council President, Gunnar Jarring of Sweden, to visit the subcontinent for the purpose of discussing the resolution with India and Pakistan.[43]

Soviet delegate, Sobolev, on 18 February, proposed an amendment to the above resolution. He argued that "the situation in Kashmir has changed considerably" since 1948,

[41] Pravda, 19 December 1961.
[42] Pravda, 22 December 1961.
[43] SCOR, 12th Sess., 768 mtg.

when the Security Council first called for a plebiscite. He urged bilateral negotiations on Kashmir by India and Pakistan "without outside intervention of any sort." In a counter-resolution Sobolev deleted reference to "the use of a temporary UN force in connection with demilitarisation" in Kashmir.[44] After the Soviet amendment was rejected Sobolev vetoed the Western-sponsored resolution on 20 February. Explaining his use of the veto, he said:

> The Charter of the United Nations, however, states clearly and unmistakably that the United Nations armed forces may be used solely for the purpose of repelling aggression and restoring international peace. The dispatch of United Nations force to permit the holding of a plebiscite in Kashmir would be contrary to the Charter and would be insulting to the national pride of the people of Kashmir.[45]

Pakistan again took the Kashmir question to the Security Council in January 1962 on the ground that the speeches of certain Indian leaders revealed a plan to recapture the portion of Kashmir under Pakistan. The Soviet delegate maintained that no new situation had arisen in Kashmir to warrant a fresh discussion by the Council. When the Irish delegate introduced a resolution urging the two governments to negotiate on the dispute at the earliest and settle it on the basis of a plebiscite the Soviet delegate vetoed it. The Soviet delegate said:

> We have already pointed out in our statement of 4 May 1962, that the resolution about this plebiscite was

[44] *Ibid.*, 770th mtg. (18 February 1957), pp. 38-40.
[45] *Ibid.*, 773rd mtg., p. 32.

adopted by the Council in quite a different set of practical circumstances and that the resolution adopted by
the United Nations Commission for India and Pakistan
rested on conditions which were prerequisite for carry-
ing out this whole plan. The most important condition
—and I must apologize for having, so to speak, to return
from Z to A, but that is not the fault of the USSR
delegation—was the preliminary withdrawal of Pakistan
troops from the entire territory of Kashmir.[46]

The Soviet and the 1962 Sino-Indian Conflict

The Sino-Indian border conflict of 1962 put Indo-
Soviet friendship to an acid test. The simultaneous erup-
tion of the Cuban crisis further complicated the Soviet
Union's difficulties. On 25 October *Pravda* published an
editorial which spoke of the "notorious McMahon Line"
and supported the Chinese proposals for the end of conflict, describing them as "constructive." The editorial
caused a near storm in India. Written after the Cuban
blockade came into effect, it aimed at seeking China's
cooperation in the biggest post-war confrontation with the
USA. As the Cuban crisis passed, the new Soviet stand
surfaced in the form of an editorial in *Pravda* on 5 November which almost amounted to ordering China to stop
fighting India. Entitled "Negotiation is the Road for
Settling the Conflict," it declared: "The bloodshed cannot
be allowed to continue."

Soviet criticism of China's policies in provoking the
Sino-Indian conflict became more explicit when the Sino-
Soviet ideological rift came into the open. Suslov made

[46] SCOR, mtg. 1016, p. 17.

a forthright criticism of China in a report to the Central Committee:

> It is a fact that when the Carribean crisis was at its height the PRC Government extended the armed conflict on the Sino-Indian frontier. No matter how the Chinese leaders try to belatedly justify their behaviour at that moment, they cannot escape their responsibility for the fact that by their actions they essentially helped the extreme reactionary circles of imperialism, thereby aggravating an already complicated and dangerous situation in the world.[47]

Before the Sino-Indian conflict, the USSR had entered into an agreement with India for the supply of a few squadrons of MiG supersonic fighters and the erection of factories to manufacture them in India. Despite speculation in certain quarters to the contrary, the Soviet supplies arrived on schedule. The first consignment of fighters arrived in February 1963. An Indian military mission went to Moscow in August 1963 to procure equipment, including missiles, to be used for India's defence against China.

Soviet Relations with Pakistan

In his Srinagar speech in December 1955 referring to the Soviet Union's friendly relations with Afghanistan Khrushchev said: "We should very much like to have similar relations with Pakistan, and it is not our fault that such relations have so far not developed." He added:

[47] New Times, No. 15, Supplement, 1964, p. 49.

"But we shall persistently strive to improve these relations in the interests of peace."[48] In his report on the tour to the Supreme Soviet, Bulganin had declared:

> We would be glad if Pakistan would also take advantage of such opportunities. The Soviet Union would like its relations with Pakistan to be no less friendly than its relations with India, Burma and Afghanistan, and it is not our fault that this is not so as yet. However, the Soviet government will continue to exert efforts to improve our relations with Pakistan.[49]

Soviet efforts to improve relations with Pakistan continued, the military alliances with the USA notwithstanding. In February 1956, Bulganin offered Pakistan technical knowhow for peaceful uses of atomic energy. On 23 March an article by K. Petrov in *Izvestia* described the proclamation of Pakistan as a republic as "an important event in the life of the country, signifying its advancement on the path of national development." The writer said that the Soviet Union "could share with Pakistan its knowledge and experience in the utilisation of atomic energy and Soviet-Pakistani trade could also develop to mutual advantage."

Pakistan's Republic Day celebrations in Moscow were attended by Foreign Minister Molotov, who hinted that the Soviet Government would be willing to construct a steel plant in Pakistan as it had done in India.[50] Vice-Chairman of the Council of Ministers, Mikoyan, attended the inauguration of the republic in Karachi and invited the Speaker of the Pakistan Constituent Assembly to bring

[48] *Pravda,* 11 December 1955.
[49] *Pravda,* 30 December 1955.
[50] *Dawn,* 25 March 1956.

a parliamentary delegation to the USSR, and this was gladly accepted.[51]

On 15 June 1956, the Soviet Government announced a gift of 16,500 tons of rice to help Pakistan tide over a food crisis. Towards the close of June the two countries concluded a trade agreement which accorded each other "the status of a most favoured nation regarding import and export and other questions." All payments by Pakistan were to be made in its own currency. The agreement was roughly on the lines of the 1953 agreement with India. To improve political relations, the Soviet Government once again invited the Prime Minister of Pakistan to visit Moscow, but, like Liaquat Ali, he chose to go to the United States. However, Sheikh Mujibur Rahman visited the USSR in 1956 as the representative of Prime Minister Suhrawardy.

Mikoyan's statements in Karachi on his visits in 1955 and 1956 are often quoted as evidence of Soviet Union's "double-faced" attitude on the Kashmir question. Malenkov's somewhat evasive reply to the London correspondent of Dawn—"We have not expressed an opinion at all on it" —is also cited in this connection. According to Sangat Singh,

> Pakistani writers have erroneously read much in these statements of Soviet leaders, that the Soviet position on Kashmir was equivocal. What the Soviet leaders wanted to achieve by diplomacy and a conciliatory attitude without altering their basic stand was an image of reasonableness with a view to influencing Pakistani public opinion.[52]

[51] New Times, No. 14, 29 March 1956, p. 31.
[52] Sangat Singh, Pakistan's Foreign Policy—An Appraisal, Bombay, 1970, p. 138.

I. A. Benedictov, who visited Pakistan in February 1958 as leader of a Soviet parliamentary delegation, told his hosts that his country was willing to give economic and technical assistance to Pakistan, mainly in agriculture, control of floods and salination, pests and land erosion.

But military coup of October 1958, which brought General Ayub Khan to power, did not create an atmosphere favourable for close Pakistan-USSR relations. Ayub Khan had been mainly instrumental in forging Pakistan's military alliance with the West. He had accompanied Prime Minister Mohammed Ali to Washington in the fall of 1953, and had gone in early 1954 to Ankara with Governor-General Ghulam Mohammed. Moscow was convinced that Washington was behind Ayub Khan's seizure of power. The Report of the Central Committee of the CPSU to the 21st Party Congress held that the military coup in Pakistan was indicative of the fact that "an attack is developing against the democratic gains of peoples who have won national independence."[53]

But Moscow persisted with friendly overtures to Pakistan. Soviet policymakers were well aware of the anti-imperialist orientation of the Pakistani masses. The ignominious defeat of the Muslim League in the 1954 elections in East Pakistan was a clear indication of popular hostility to the policy of alignment. Pakistan's willingness to be a sponsor of the Bandung Conference was also interpreted as a hopeful sign in Moscow. Obviously, the Pakistani leaders had at times to heed the wishes of the people. Keeping all this in view Soviet planners of foreign policy set themselves the goal of establishing friendly relations with their country's southern Muslim neighbours. Khrushchev had

[53] *Pravda*, 28 January 1959.

told the Supreme Soviet in December 1955 that Moscow was willing "to meet Pakistan halfway in establishing friendly relations."[54] And "meeting halfway" meant striving for normal neighbourly relations even while the military alliances with the USA existed. The report of the Central Committee of the CPSU presented to the 20th Congress clearly stated:

> The Soviet Union will continue to strive unswervingly for the extension and strengthening of friendship and cooperation with the eastern countries.... We also believe that Iran, Turkey and Pakistan will realise that normal relations with the USSR are in their vital interests.... We are of the opinion that even under present conditions, when military alignments exist, the opportunities for improving relations between countries, particularly between neighbours, have by no means been completely exhausted. In this connection the significance of non-aggression treaties or treaties of friendship, whose conclusion would help remove existing suspicion and mistrust in relations between countries and normalise the international situation, should be emphasised. For its part, the Soviet Union is prepared to conclude such treaties.[55]

Soviet efforts to normalize relations with Pakistan continued even after the military coup in 1958, at which the Soviets looked with great suspicion. The Soviet Ambassador declared: "Only 10 per cent of the problems between the Soviet Union and Pakistan are controversial in nature, and on the remaining 90 per cent there is a possibility of

54 *Pravda*, 30 December 1955.
55 *New Times*, No. 8, 16 February 1956 (Documents), p. 19.

developing friendly relations."[56] Just a month after Ayub Khan assumed power, the Soviet Union offered help to explore natural resources, particularly oil. The two countries concluded a barter agreement in December 1959.

Pakistan's relations with the Soviet Union were at their very nadir after the shooting down of an American U-2 spyplane over Russia in May 1960. The plane, which took off from Turkey, had also touched the American airbase at Peshawar before intruding into Soviet airspace. The Soviet Union sent a strong note of protest to Pakistan, containing the warning that "if such actions are repeated from Pakistani territory it will be compelled to take proper retaliatory measures."[57] The Soviet threat helped bring an element of realism into Pakistan's policy, and the rulers of Pakistan realized that their country would be a prime target of striking power in a global war, for the Soviet Union almost touched Pakistan's northern border while the USA was thousands of miles away. Pakistan accordingly informed Washington that in future American aircraft would be able to use Pakistani airfields only after their further destination was made known in advance.[58]

The Soviet Union and Pakistan continued to conduct negotiations on Soviet technical assistance for exploration of oil and other mineral resources even during the tension after the U-2 incident. Pakistan announced acceptance of the Soviet offer in August 1960. Negotiations started in Karachi in September 1960 and were almost complete before the departure of Z. A. Bhutto, Pakistan's Minister for Natural Resources, for Moscow in December 1960.

[56] Pakistan Times, 13 June 1959.
[57] Asian Recorder, 1960, pp. 3376-7.
[58] Dawn, 15 May 1960.

In January 1961, the Soviet Union gave a long-term loan of $ 30 million for oil exploration in Pakistan.

In January 1963, the Soviet Premier received Zafrullah Khan and reiterated the Soviet desire to improve relations with Pakistan.[59] The oil agreement was followed by a barter deal in August 1963 and an air agreement in October 1963. Three more agreements on trade, economic cooperation, and cultural exchange were signed in April 1965.

President Ayub Khan's visit to the Soviet Union the same month was the first direct personal contact in 18 years between the top leaders of Pakistan and the Soviet Union. Later, Ayub Khan summed up his talks with the Soviet leaders in these words:

> I think there was general recognition on both sides that the meeting might prove a turning-point in our relations and that there were tremendous possibilities of cooperation. I found the Soviet leaders extremely knowledgable. They were courteous, polite and hospitable, but firm on their basic assumptions. I ventured to think they recognised our sincerity and came to have a better appreciation of our position.[60]

The joint communique issued at the end of the visit said there was a "frank exchange of opinion" on a broad range of topics. "Included in the talks were not only various aspects of Soviet-Pakistani relations and how they might be improved but also basic international issues,

---

59 Pakistan Horizon, 1963, p. 287.
60 Mohammad Ayub Khan, Friends Not Masters: A Political Autobiography, London, 1967, p. 173.

including the question of maintaining world peace, easing international tension, and settling international conflicts." The communique stressed the conviction of both sides that "prevention of the spread of nuclear weapons in any form whatsoever and the creation of atom-free zones in various regions" were important at that stage.[61]

The replacement of Khrushchev by "the Brezhnev-Kosygin team" in October 1964 and Ayub Khan's visit resulted in a spurt of shift-watching exercises by a host of Indian and Western scholars and in the emergence of high-sounding theories to explain the "new," "equidistant," "neutral," and "non-partisan" posture of the new Soviet leaders towards India. The sincere and persistent Soviet efforts to establish normal good-neighbourly relations with Pakistan from 1949 onwards and the potentially strong anti-imperialist forces in Pakistan have been largely ignored by many specialists in Soviet and Pakistan affairs. Thus Werner Levi writes that the Soviet-Pakistani *detente* "resulted not so much from positive measures in Soviet-Pakistan relations as from growing Pakistani dissatisfaction with American policies and actions."[62]

An Indian scholar, Mohammed Ayoob, thinks that there were "two major and interrelated reasons which prompted it [the Soviet Union] to make various overtures to Pakistan: the growing *detente* between the Soviet Union and the United States and the growing conflict and friction between the Soviet Union and Communist China."[63]

[61] *Pravda*, 11 April 1965.

[62] Werner Levi, "Pakistan, the Soviet Union and China," *Pacific Affairs*, Vol. 35, 1962, p. 217.

[63] Mohammed Ayoob, "Pakistan's Soviet Policy, 1950-1968: A Balance Sheet" in M. S. Rajan (ed.), *Studies in Politics*, Delhi, 1971, p. 235. According to Ayoob, the modification in the

Ayoob, surely, is familiar with the Soviet "overtures" to Pakistan at a much earlier period, when there were no signs of the so-called Soviet-American *detente* and when there was no rift between China and the Soviet Union.

Another Indian specialist on Soviet affairs, R. Vaidyanath, refers to New Delhi's "anxiety" that the Soviet Union "far from trying to assuage India's feelings, has started exhibiting a marked insensitivity to them."[64] However, after a detailed analysis of "subtle" Soviet appeasement of Pakistan and the "tightrope-walking" by the Soviet Union in its policy towards the Indo-Pakistani subcontinent, Vaidyanath has ultimately found "ample evidence to indicate that the Soviet Union has always

Soviet policy towards India and Pakistan "was more in the style than in the substance" (p. 240).

[64] R. Vaidyanath, "Recent Trends in Soviet Politics Towards India and Pakistan," *International Studies*, Bombay, Vol VII, No. 3, January 1966. As examples of this "insensitivity" of the Soviets towards India's feelings, Vaidyanath cites Mikoyan's suggestion on his visit to New Delhi in June 1964 "that it was time for India and Pakistan to seek a settlement of all their differences" and the August 1965 remark of Soviet Vice-Premier K. Mazurov in New Delhi "that the Soviet Union should not be expected to allow its relations with India and Pakistan to be governed by the mutual relations of these two countries." "This hardening of Soviet attitude towards India" (an inference the author strangely draws from these two innocuous and well-intentioned statements, the second being from August 1965), writes Vaidyanath, "led India to seek a renewed assurance from the Soviet Union during Radhakrishnan's visit to Moscow in September 1964 (!) that Moscow would not turn a blind eye to India's vital interests in its dealings with Pakistan" (p. 437).

shown a marked preference, for India."[65] But, as the foregoing survey of Soviet policies towards India and Pakistan has shown, a competitive approach to these two countries is alien to Soviet thinking. The Soviet Union desires to be friendly with both of them and never tried to incite one against the other. It was not its fault if Pakistan did not clasp the proffered hand of friendship, which India not only grasped but sought.

[65] *Ibid.*, p. 444. Similarly J. A. Naik thinks that "there is reason to believe that India still continues to be a more valuable partner for the Soviets" and that "Indo-Soviet partnership is bound to be closer than the Soviet-Pakistani companionship (*op. cit.*, p. 147). In the opinion of Maya Kulkarni, though a "shift" in Soviet policy on Kashmir was noticeable, yet "it did not entail a fundamental change in Indo-Soviet relations." According to her, to the Soviet leaders "close Indo-Soviet relations appear crucial to the preservation of balance of power in Asia" (Maya Kulkarni, *Indo-Soviet Political Relations*, Bombay, 1968, pp. 122-3, 127).

On the other hand, V. S. Budhraj holds that "the support given to India was not unqualified and unambiguous and that the Kremlin was not so firmly behind India on this issue (of Kashmir) as it was understood in New Delhi" (*op. cit.*, p. 20). He feels that the Indian subcontinent is becoming involved in the Sino-Soviet power struggle (p. 37). Another scholar, Harish Kapur, finds the "shift" in Soviet attitude towards India quite "apparent." But he thinks that this does not mean that Moscow has ceased to consider India an "important objective" of Soviet diplomacy. Kapur writes: "Far from it, India was still considered important and economic and military assistance continued to flow as before. Only Pakistan was no longer considered an enemy" ("The Shift in Soviet Attitude Towards India," *Indo-Soviet Relations*, Bombay, p. 4).

CHAPTER V

BRIDGING THE GULF: TASHKENT

BY 1965 THE SOVIET UNION HAD ACHIEVED CONSIDERABLE success in its long-cherished aim of establishing an understanding with Pakistan without prejudicing the decade-old cordial relations with India. Ayub Khan's visit to Moscow in April was followed by Lal Bahadur Shastri's in May, indicating the great importance the Soviet Union attached to ties with India and a desire to strengthen them further. The Soviet leaders declared publicly that the Soviet-Pakistani *detente* did not involve any sacrifice of India's interests. Kosygin put it thus in his speech at the Kremlin reception for Shastri: "When the Soviet Union is striving to improve its relations with a third country this does not have to be at the cost of Soviet-Indian friendship."[1]

The Soviet policy of friendship with both India and Pakistan was put to severe tests during 1965, but it emerged successfully with added confidence and trust. When a crisis arose over the Rann of Kutch in April-May 1965 the Soviet Union appealed to India and Pakistan to resolve it through direct negotiations.[2] The Soviet stand con-

[1] *Pravda*, 16 May 1965.
[2] *Pravda*, 9 May 1965.

tained nothing new. On Kashmir too, the Soviet Union had always favoured a bilateral approach. It was forced to veto the Western proposals in 1957 and 1962 as they favoured internationalization of the question and its solution by the induction of foreign troops.

In February 1964, when Pakistan again raised the Kashmir question in the Security Council, the Soviet delegate in his speech, while stating clearly his country's position "that the question of Kashmir's belonging to India has already been decided by the Kashmiri people," also said:

The Soviet delegation is firmly of the opinion that the India-Pakistan dispute should be settled directly by the parties concerned[3]—India and Pakistan—and, of course, exclusively by peaceful means. The parties to this dispute are themselves capable of taking steps to relax the tensions which exist between them. We should like to point out, with special emphasis, that this requires a calm and normal atmosphere.[4]

If this attitude of the Soviet Union in 1964 towards the dispute between India and Pakistan is compared with its

[3] The British approach as A. Appadorai pinpointed in his Lal Bahadur Shastri Memorial Lecture on the Tashkent Declaration at the Birla Institute of Technology and Science, Pilani, in February 1969, had strongly disfavoured any direct talks between India and Pakistan to settle their dispute. When the Dixon report, which recommended that the parties settle the matter between themselves came up for discussion before the Security Council on 21 February 1957, the British representative, Gladwyn Jebb, took the stand that his government could not accept Dixon's view. (A. Appadorai, *The Tashkent Declaration*. 1969, p. 11.)

[4] SCOR, 1090th mtg., 14 February 1964, paras 50-51.

attitude at the time of the conflict over the Rann of Kutch a year later, nothing but a marked consistency meets the eye, however critical. Yet it is regrettable that some Indian writers have chosen to overlook this and instead claim that "an increase in Pakistani aggressiveness against India" was, "an almost inevitable outcome of Soviet 'neutrality' between India and Pakistan"[5] in the Kutch dispute.

If the Indo-Pakistani conflict of September 1965 was, as alleged, an "inevitable outcome" of the Soviet "neutrality" in the Kutch dispute (as evidenced by Soviet insistence on a solution of differences through direct negotiations), one wonders why the Kutch conflict cannot be said to have arisen from the Soviet stand on Kashmir in February 1964 "that the India-Pakistan dispute should be settled directly by the parties concerned." It is not without significance that the old mouthpiece of British colonialism, The Times of London, should have initiated the theory of "changing" Russian policy in regard to the subcontinent. The Soviet statement on the Kutch conflict was characterized by this newspaper as "significant" and "surprising." It went on to comment:

It goes to confirm that Russia's policy on the subcontinent is changing, turning from its previous out-and-out commitment to India's case over Kashmir and everything else at issue with Pakistan to a more wary and detached stance between the two neighbours. Perhaps even to non-alignment.[6]

[5] See R. Vaidyanath, op. cit., pp. 437-8.
[6] The Times, 10 May 1965.

In September 1965, when a big armed conflict flared up between India and Pakistan, Kosygin sent messages to both Ayub Khan and Lal Bahadur Shastri pleading for the "immediate cessation of military operations."[7] Kosygin declared emphatically: "In the present grave situation, the main emphasis should not be placed on the question of the cause of the conflict or of ascertaining who is right and who is wrong. The main efforts should be concentrated...on halting the tanks and silencing the guns."[8] He expressed the willingness of the Soviet Government to lend its good offices in this matter if the parties so desired.

During the debate in the Security Council on the fighting in Kashmir, the Soviet delegate again almost repeated the stand of a bilateral solution by peaceful means which the Soviet Union had taken in 1964, and declared:

We consider it necessary to point out that any further exacerbation of the conflict in Kashmir might further aggravate tension on the Asian continent. That is why, at this time, we should like to express our confidence that, above all, India and Pakistan themselves will find a way to put an immediate end to the bloodshed in Kashmir and halt this conflict. The two neighbouring states must resolve the outstanding issues between them by peaceful means, with due regard for their mutual interests.[9]

The stand taken by the Soviet Union during the conflict and after coincided with the Indian approach of giving priority to the urgent task of ending recourse to

[7] *Pravda*, 12 September 1965.
[8] *Ibid.*
[9] SCOR, yr. 20, mtg. 1237, 4 September 1965, pp. 36-7.

arms for the solution of a specific dispute. The Soviet delegate told the Security Council on 18 September that the fighting between India and Pakistan was "an ominous threat to international security" and added:

It is quite obvious that such a turn of events is not at all in the interests of the peoples of India and Pakistan or the peoples of Asia as a whole.... It is equally clear that the continuation of this conflict benefits only the forces which are pursuing the criminal policy of dividing peoples so as to achieve their imperialist and expansionist aims.[10]

He explained that the Soviet "concern" at the India-Pakistan armed conflict represented "above all the sincere and disinterested feelings of friends of the peoples of India and Pakistan for peace to be restored between the two countries." The Soviet Union was, he frankly admitted, also concerned "because the hostilities are taking place in a region immediately adjacent to the frontiers of the Soviet Union."[11]

He said the Soviet attitude was determined "by the general lines of the peaceloving foreign policy" by their "profound conviction that when disputes arise between states—whatever their origin—they should be settled by peaceful means, by negotiations."

Although the Soviet delegate did not openly contradict Ayub Khan, who in his reply connected a ceasefire with the evolution of effective machinery to settle the Kashmir

[10] SCOR, yr. 20, mtg. 1241, 18 September 1965, pp. 25-8.
[11] Ibid.

dispute finally, he took notice of Shastri's willingness to
order a ceasefire as soon as Pakistan agreed and emphasized
the need for an immediate end to the armed conflict.[12]
He said:

It has become more clear than ever that the main task
now is to achieve an immediate cessation of hostilities
between India and Pakistan and to put an end to the
bloodshed. The deafening roar of guns and thunder of
bombs are obstructing negotiations.... In an atmosphere of armed conflict it is hardly possible to solve
the problems which exist between the two states, and
their solution is most desirable in the interests of good-
neighbourly relations between them.

It goes without saying that it is first and foremost the
Governments of India and Pakistan themselves which
can and must settle the present conflict. The Charter of
the UN and the Bandung principles cry out for states-
man-like wisdom on the part of the leaders of both countries.[13]

Again when on 25 October Bhutto tried to raise in the
Security Council the Indian "terror" against the Jammu
and Kashmir people, quoting reports in the Le Figaro,
Newsweek, Daily Telegraph and the New York Times,
the Soviet delegate emphasized:

Now the main task is to consolidate the ceasefire, to
ensure strict and scrupulous observance of the ceasefire

[12]Ibid.
[13] Ibid. Pakistan, supported by Jordan, wanted a ceasefire, a
withdrawal and a solution of the Kashmir question to be given
the same emphasis.

agreement and to take the next step towards strengthening peace between India and Pakistan. The withdrawal by both sides to the August 5, 1965 position must proceed more rapidly.... These are the questions that must be settled first.[14]

The Soviet Union also maintained its opposition to the introduction of foreign troops in Kashmir up to the last. On 25 October and 5 November the Soviet representative objected to the Secretary-General's expansion, without reference to the Security Council, of the UN Military Observers' Group in India and Pakistan by assigning senior NATO officers under the cover of implementing Resolution No 210 of the Security Council of 6 September 1965.[15] The basic Soviet stand on Kashmir's accession to India, too, remained unchanged. Both in the *Pravda* statement of 24 August 1965, and in the speech of the Soviet delegate in the Security Council on 4 September 1965, Kashmir was referred to as "the Indian State of Jammu and Kashmir."[16] But, as the Soviet Union was deeply interested in preserving peace on the subcontinent, it refrained from blaming either side for starting the conflict as this would only have aggravated the matter.

A survey of the Soviet stand on the Indo-Pakistani conflict, as reflected in the numerous articles, commentaries and statements of leaders published in the Soviet press, throws interesting light on the genuine concern for peace and good-neighbourly relations between the people of India and Pakistan, whom Brezhnev called "blood brothers" at the Soviet-Rumanian friendship meeting in

[14] SCOR, yr. 20, 1247 mtg., 25 October 1965, p. 49.
[15] Ibid., p. 50, 58.
[16] SCOR, yr. 20, mtg. 1237, 4 September 1965, p. 35.

Moscow.[17] The *Pravda* article of 24 August entitled "Stop Bloodshed in Kashmir" called Kashmir a "grim colonial legacy" which the "imperialists have more than once tried to use to put the peoples of India and Pakistan at loggerheads."

A Tass statement of 7 September 1965 offered Soviet "good offices" to both India and Pakistan, if they deemed them useful, to restore peace in the area. Tass said Soviet concern was increasing as the conflict was taking place in an area neighbouring its frontiers.[18] In a commentary on Moscow Television, I. Belyaev of the Afro-Asian Department of the *Pravda* made a passionate plea for ending the conflict "as it is a war between two peoples who were one people and lived in one country, India, before it was divided in 1947." "People of India and Pakistan," Belyaev added, "must not allow outside forces to use religion to play one against the other to serve their own vested interests."[19]

When the Chinese through their note of 8 September to India tried to instigate Pakistan by holding out a threat to India, the Soviet Union condemned the Chinese action. Brezhnev's warning of 11 September against "third forces" which tried to benefit by the aggravation of India-Pakistan relations and "sometimes added fuel to the fire" was clearly addressed to China. In his speech before the Rumanian leaders he made a warm and friendly reference to India. Brezhnev said:

Bonds of friendship which have already become traditional exist between us and India. We are accustomed

[17] *Pravda*, 11 September 1965.
[18] *Pravda*, 8 September 1965.
[19] Cited by Bhagat Vats, *Foreign Intrigues Against India*, New Delhi, 1967, p. 137.

to appreciate and respect India's peaceloving foreign policy, her fidelity to the principles of non-alignment, national freedom and friendly international cooperation.

Referring to Pakistan, he said:

We want to develop good neighbourly relations with Pakistan as well . . . and we have noted with satisfaction that this striving of ours met with understanding on the part of the Pakistani Government.[20]

Brezhnev appealed to the leaders of India and Pakistan to show realism, restraint and wisdom and quench the war flames immediately by ordering a ceasefire and withdrawing their troops to the positions they held before fighting commenced. The Tass statement of 13 September 1965, again warned those who by "their incendiary statements" aggravated the India-Pakistan conflict.[21] While indirectly condemning the Chinese, the Tass statement also attacked the "forces of imperialism and reaction" which wanted to reimpose the yoke of colonialism and neo-colonialism on the liberated peoples. It stated: "Even now American imperialism is trying to exploit the military clashes between India and Pakistan, to divert peoples' attention from the United States' course in Vietnam." The Tass statement asserted that there was no possibility for settling the conflict other than by peaceful means. These statements were a hint that India could count on Soviet support in the event of a serious situation developing on India's borders as a result of intervention

---

[20] Pravda, 11 September, 1965.
[21] Pravda, 14 September 1965.

by a third party.

A Soviet weekly, Za Rubezhom, also criticized the Chinese action.[22] The Soviet political weekly, New Times, carried an article by D. Volski arguing that the conflict over Kashmir did not spring from the composition of the population of that state, as the West claimed, but from the policy of British colonialism. Volsky wrote that it was because of Britain's efforts that "Kashmir became a bone of contention between the two new states."[23] New Times again reverted to this theme in a long article entitled "Kashmir Conflict: Some Antecedents" which clearly stated that this issue had been "aggravated all along by imperialist interference and intrigue."[24] The USA, it said, had become Britain's senior partner in exploiting the Kashmir question.

The weekly said that the USA and its allies had tabled resolution after resolution in the Security Council with the general idea that under the cover of conducting a plebiscite, troops of the Western powers could be brought into Kashmir and stationed there indefinitely. "The ultimate purpose was to have Kashmir ruled for years to come by an American governor." New Times said that when India turned down this neo-colonialist proposal, Washington produced a plan for an "independent" Kashmir under American aegis. The weekly published a facsimile of the front page of the New York Times of 5 July 1953, showing a map of partitioned Kashmir with the valley as an independent state. By the summer of 1953, the Soviet weekly said, preparations for a separatist putsch were almost complete, but the Indian authorities

[22] Bhagat Vats, op. cit., p. 147.
[23] New Times, 17 September 1965.
[24] Ibid., 13 October 1965.

stepped in time by taking into custody local politicians suspected of complicity. It also blamed the USA for pressurizing India in 1962, taking advantage of the Sino-Indian border conflict.

A Soviet assessment of the Kashmir question was also published in the *Literaturnaya Gazeta* of 27 October 1965. The writer, S. Mikoyan, son of former President Anastas Mikoyan (often quoted as having taken in Karachi a "non-committal" attitude towards India's claim to Kashmir), said that India had to take "defensive action by proceeding towards Lahore to divert Pakistani forces." He accused Mountbatten of having engineered the idea of a plebiscite and accepted the legal validity of Kashmir's accession to India. Mikoyan explained the Soviet stand on Kashmir in the broad perspective of Anglo-American conspiracy to use Pakistan to put pressure on India for their imperialist ends. The issue could be settled only by the two countries without the intervention of third parties, he emphasized.

As a power deeply interested in peace and stability on the Indian subcontinent, the Soviet Union took initiative to bring the two warring nations to the negotiating table. The Soviet Premier followed his letter of 20 August by letters of 4, 11 and 17 September. Shastri consented, though it took some time before Pakistan agreed to meet in Tashkent. The meeting finally took place from 3 January to 10 January 1966.

The choice of Tashkent as the meeting place was very happy. The conference between the Indian and Pakistani leaders took place on Asian soil in an ancient city whose history and culture are indissolubly linked with those of the two countries. The congenial atmosphere created by the citizens of Tashkent for the success of the conference must not be underestimated. Both the Indian and Pakistani negotiators appreciated the cordiality shown to them.

All this, however, did not mean that the conference proceeded smoothly. On the contrary, it ran a very complicated course and its outcome was difficult to foresee right up to the closing day. If the conference succeeded, this was in a large measure due to the great pains taken by Premier Kosygin to bring the two sides closer. As M. S. Rajan has written:

> ... the Soviet Prime Minister firmly stuck to the letter and spirit of the offer of good offices. He did not make at any stage any proposals, or pressurise either of the leaders to accept the proposals of the other. Contrary to inspired and malicious press reports, there was no Soviet armtwisting of India or Pakistan. All that the Soviet Prime Minister tried to do was to bring to bear on the two leaders his tremendous powers of persuasion to make them see each other's point of view in the interest of peace in the Indian subcontinent.[25]

Kosygin made a very significant contribution to bring about agreement between the Indian and Pakistani leaders on the declaration which was eventually signed by them on 10 January.

Many circles in the West, as well as the Chinese, were obviously not happy at the Tashkent meeting. The *Daily Telegraph* of London wrote: "... it is at least odd and thought-provoking that when two Commonwealth coun-

[25] M. S. Rajan, "The Tashkent Declaration: Retrospect and Prospect," *International Studies*, Vol. 8, July 1966-April 1967, p. 8.

tries fall out it is Russia which steps forward as an inter-
mediary."[26] The *Guardian* commented:

> Their [Western powers'] detachment (!) has been fatal.
> Had they given their backing to either India or Pakistan,
> the Kashmir dispute might have been settled long ago,
> and they would not have incurred the hostility of both
> sides.... By their neutrality they have driven Pakistan
> into the arms of China, and they may yet drive India
> into the arms of Russia.[27]

Similarly, the *Sunday Telegraph* wrote,

> That President Ayub and Mr Shastri should be plan-
> ning to settle their quarrel not in London, not in
> Ottawa, not in Canberra, not even in Washington but
> in Tashkent is a new fact for every believer in Common-
> wealth to ponder.[28]

British journalists covering the Tashkent meeting were
openly sceptical about its success. One of them is said
to have remarked to a Soviet journalist: "We tried to
reconcile them for 250 years, and in vain; but you are
hoping to do this in two or three days." Prime Minister
Wilson's release of his correspondence with Noel Baker
on the origins of the Indo-Pakistan conflict, and the
Chinese note to India during the Tashkent conference
were indirect moves to make it difficult for the parties
to come to an understanding.

The nine-clause Tashkent Declaration signed by Shastri

[26] *The Daily Telegraph*, 13 September 1965.
[27] *The Guardian*, 13 September 1965.
[28] *The Sunday Telegraph*, 26 September 1965.

and Ayub Khan and witnessed by Kosygin had a twofold object—firstly, the immediate resumption of normal, friendly relations between India and Pakistan, and, secondly, to evolve a procedure for the settlement of all disputes between the two countries through peaceful means.

Shastri felt that the declaration had achieved "very tangible results." In a private conversation with Defence Minister Y. B. Chavan soon after signing it, he uttered the memorable words: "We have fought in this [Indo-Pakistan conflict] with all our strength. Now we have to fight for peace with all our strength." Kosygin expressed the hope that the declaration might become "the symbol of eternal friendship between India and Pakistan" and would also "strengthen friendship between India and the Soviet Union and between Pakistan and the Soviet Union." He also told newsmen that the declaration "lays down the real foundations for the creation of conditions of peace in this most important area of Asia."[29] It was "a new stage in the development of relations between India and Pakistan."

The Tashkent Declaration found wide support among the people and Government of India. The Soviet Union's role at the conference was highly appreciated. On the first anniversary of the declaration, M. C. Chagla, the then foreign Minister, evaluated the Soviet efforts thus:

The Soviet Union's only concern was the cause of peace and overpowering necessity for the establishment

[29] *Soviet Review* (New Delhi, Information Deptt. of the USSR Embassy), 14 January 1966.

of friendly relations between the two neighbouring countries in the subcontinent of India.[30]

In her address to the Soviet-Indian Friendship Society, Moscow, Prime Minister Indira Gandhi on 14 July 1966 said:

We desire the friendship of Pakistan. We are sincerely anxious to abide by the Tashkent Declaration, which binds both parties to abjure the use of force. We seek economic and other cooperation with Pakistan in a manner consistent with the honour and interest of both countries. We have extended the hand of friendship to Pakistan and hope that they will no longer hesitate to grasp it.[31]

Speaking before the General Assembly of the UN, Foreign Minister Swaran Singh described the declaration as "a new framework" in which normal and friendly relations between the two countries would be restored. He said:

The underlying concept of the declaration was the deep conviction that peaceful relations between India and Pakistan are vital for the maintenance of their political independence and the achievement of their economic and social development. If all the provisions of the declaration are implemented faithfully in letter and spirit, an atmosphere will be created in which all differ-

[30] The Tashkent Declaration, First Anniversary: January 10, 1967, Publications Division, Govt. of India, New Delhi, 1967, p. 1.
[31] Ibid., pp. 7-8.

ences between the two countries can be settled peacefully.[32]

A similar response to the declaration from the Pakistani leaders has unfortunately been wanting. Yet even there in his first of the month broadcast of February 1966, Ayub Khan chided its critics in the following words:

True, we were not able to resolve this dispute [Kashmir] in an acceptable manner. But who could expect that a problem which had been hanging fire for the last 18 years would be resolved in a single meeting....

World opinion has seen in the Tashkent Declaration an opening for the peaceful settlement of the dispute of Jammu and Kashmir. But there are some people in our country who are not prepared to accept this. Perhaps they see war as the only means of the settlement of this dispute. Perhaps they believe that since we had war once we should have it all the time. The issues of peace and war are not decided in the heat of emotion but by cold logic and cool thinking. The sentiments of people must be respected under all circumstances. But the interests of people come first. They cannot be sacrificed and no responsible person will do that.... It is my belief that the Tashkent Declaration not only strengthens the integrity of Pakistan but also provides a possibility for the peaceful settlement of the dispute of Jammu and Kashmir.

This possibility can be turned into reality if India and Pakistan stop this sterile discussion of who won and who lost, recognise that the future of the people of the

---

[32] Ibid., p. 8.

subcontinent lies in peace.... Therein lies the welfare of India, therein lies the welfare of Pakistan.[33]

Denigration of the declaration started in certain influential circles in the West, especially in Britain. *The Times* of London initiated the controversy, later picked up by the several Pakistani leaders and high government officials, that the agreement was only a no-force declaration. On the morrow of its adoption this newspaper wrote: "This is far from the no-war declaration that would have assured the Indians that Kashmir was closed to future violence."[34] Michael Edwardes, in an article published in the journal of the Royal Institute of International Affairs, described Tashkent as "a negative achievement" and called the declaration a "funerary monument to the dead Prime Minister."[35] He wrote: "The dialogue he had begun, instead of continuing fruitfully, petrified into an obituary." Alastair Lamb described the Tashkent spirit as "a phrase of little meaning"[36] and suggested a partition of Jammu and Kashmir along communal lines. China, which had desired the dispute between India and Pakistan to be prolonged, called Tashkent "a neo-colonialist gathering" and belittled the significance of the declaration.

Some official circles in Pakistan were openly critical. Bhutto, who accompanied Ayub Khan to Tashkent, quit the Cabinet and made it publicly known that he did not approve of the agreement. Later, when he formed an opposition party, he called Tashkent a betrayal of Pakis-

---

[33] *Dawn*, 2 February 1966.
[34] *The Times*, 11 January 1966.
[35] *International Affairs*, London, Vol. 42, No. 3, July 1966.
[36] Alastair Lamb, *Crisis in Kashmir, 1947 to 1966*, London, 1966, p. 137, 149.

tani interests. Altaf Gauhar, Secretary to the Pakistani
Ministry of Information and Broadcasting, in a speech at
the Pakistan Institute of International Affairs loudly re-
pudiated the view that by reaffirming Pakistan's obliga-
tions under the UN Charter not to have recourse to force
it had in effect entered into a no-war pact with India.
He tried to put a fanciful gloss on the Charter by his
peculiar interpretation that it permitted Pakistan even to
resort to war over the Kashmir issue if it was not solved
peacefully.

All these misinterpretations of the declaration and the
Charter need not be taken seriously as they were perhaps
necessitated by the need to assuage popular expectations
in Pakistan that in view of the allegedly great victories
of the Pakistani Army it would get complete satisfaction
for its demands on India, in particular a favourable settlement on Kashmir.[37] In the more populous part of
Pakistan, the eastern wing, the declaration was welcomed
from the start.[38] A leading newspaper of East Pakistan,
Sangbad of Dacca, in an article on the first anniversary of
Tashkent stated:

> The historic Tashkent Declaration signed on 10 Janu-
> ary last is a priceless treasure of 600 million people.
> The Tashkent Declaration has presented us with a
> solid foundation, a great ideal and correct directive to
> build a happy, prosperous, peaceful and democratic
> future and also to restore friendly relations between
> the two peoples of this subcontinent.... The greatest
> achievements of the Tashkent Declaration are the re-

[37] M. S. Rajan, op. cit., p. 16.
[38] G. W. Choudhury, *Pakistan's Relation with India 1947-
1966*, London, 1968, p. 303.

jection of principle of war and use of force as the means to settle interstate disputes, acceptance of the principle of peaceful negotiations and indispensability of Indo-Pak friendship.[39]

The Soviet Union's approach to the declaration has nothing in common with its misinterpretation in certain quarters in Pakistan. In his letters of 4 September 1965, to Prime Minister Shastri and President Ayub Khan, Kosygin clearly stated: "We are deeply convinced... that any disputes, *including questions connected with Kashmir*, can best be settled by peaceful means only. The military way cannot lead to their solution"[40] (emphasis added).

New Times, in a special article to mark the third anniversary of the *Tashkent* declaration, took note of the opposition to it from "the chauvinistically minded elements in both countries" and commented:

Characteristically enough, they have in effect been joined by Peking instigated "Leftists." In Pakistan, for instance, they marked the third anniversary of the Taskent Declaration by sharply attacking it and issuing provocatory appeals for an "armed liberation struggle" in Kashmir.[41]

Whatever its critics might say, the declaration opened a new chapter in Indo-Pakistani relations. It normalized,

[39] Cited by B. L. Sharma, *The Kashmir Story*, Bombay, 1967, p. 218.
[40] Dev Sharma, *Tashkent: A Study in Foreign Relations with Documents*, Allahabad, 1966, pp. 105-6
[41] *New Times*, 22 January 1969, p. 7.

at a minimum formal level, relations between the two states, which had fought two undeclared wars in the course of one year. Some immediate gains of the declaration may be recounted. All armed personnel of the two countries were withdrawn before 25 February 1966, to the positions they held before 5 August 1965. The normal functioning of diplomatic missions was restored with the return of the High Commissioners to their respective posts in New Delhi and Rawalpindi. Communications between the two countries, disrupted by the war were restored, interstate travel was allowed through two points on the common land border, and the cargo and ships seized during the war were returned. Prisoners of war were also exchanged. Resumption of trade, and cultural relations has been slow, primarily because Pakistan has taken the view that meaningful talks on Kashmir are essential for such normalization.

The Tashkent Declaration envisaged joint meetings at ministerial and other levels and the setting up of joint Indo-Pakistani bodies to consider problems of common concern. But the ministerial talks at Rawalpindi in March 1966 did not result in substantial progress though the joint communique issued at their end stated: "Considerable progress was made in clarifying the issues involved. The talks, which were of an exploratory nature, led to a useful exchange of views."[42] Procedural agreement has since been arrived at for consideration of the Farakka Barrage dispute,[43] and fair progress has been made in demarcating boundaries in the eastern sector.

[42] Dev Sharma, op. cit., p. 121.
[43] According to Pakistani writer, Mukhtar Zaman, who was present in New Delhi when the Indo-Pak negotiations on the Farakka Barrage took place, the Soviet Ambassador used his

"But" as the Soviet weekly *New Times* wrote, "the path to the establishment of good neighbourly relations between India and Pakistan is still beset by difficulties both objective, due to survivals of old disagreements, and subjective, created by irresponsible elements and political forces which are not interested in peace and stability in Hindustan. The people and Governments of India and Pakistan will have to exert much efforts to implement the provisions of the Tashkent Declaration, which is the only instrument capable of settling their differences and promoting truly good-neighbourly relations."[44]

"The Tashkent spirit", wrote Romesh Chandra, Secretary-General of the World Peace Council, "can be carried forward only with the active and conscious intervention of the people."[45] Whatever may be the immediate response from Pakistan, India should continue to take new initiatives for the solution of the problems, as sooner or later this will evoke a sympathetic response from the democratic forces and people of Pakistan. The complete rout of obscurantist forces in the recent general elections in Pakistan raises the hope that given sincere efforts Indo-Pakistani relations can be established on an even keel.

In the post-Tashkent period the Soviet Union, as before, has been striving hard to develop close relations with both India and Pakistan and to utilize every opportunity to bridge their differences. The year 1966 saw a marked

---

good offices to keep them going. See *Pakistan Horizon*, V. 22, No. 2, 1969, p. 133.

[44] *New Times*, 22 January 1969, p. 7.

[45] Romesh Chandra, *The Tashkent Spirit*, New Delhi, 1966, pp. 12-3.

increase in Soviet contacts with Pakistan. In January, a Soviet-Pakistani barter agreement was signed, providing for the exchange of Pakistani rice for Russian vehicles and roadbuilding and engineering machinery.[46] In May, Mazurov headed a nine-member Soviet parliamentary delegation to Pakistan. A contract was signed in Dacca with the Soviet Union for the construction of a thermal power station in Gorzala, East Pakistan, with a capacity of 110,000 kilowatts.[47] In mid-1966, when Pakistan was thinking of reviving the Kashmir question in the Security Council, N. P. Firyubin paid an urgent visit to Pakistan with a message from Kosygin invoking the Tashkent spirit.[48]

Soviet visitors to Pakistan have repeatedly stressed the theme of the Tashkent Declaration. Prof. Gherman Sverglov, of the Institute of World Economy and International Relations, Moscow, who visited Pakistan in November 1966, said the Kashmir problem should be tackled in accordance with the interests of the people of the India-Pakistan subcontinent.[49] Later, the leader of a Soviet trade union delegation to Pakistan, G. Podelshikov, made the same plea, namely that a solution in Kashmir should be sought through consultation by the people of Kashmir, Pakistan, and India without outside intervention.[50]

The Soviet Union stepped up economic aid to Pakistan. Towards the end of 1966 it offered $ 80 million in aid. It also agreed to grant a credit of Rs 600 million to Pakistan for constructing 15 broadcasting stations.

[46] Dawn, 19 January 1966.
[47] Sangat Singh, op. cit., p. 151.
[48] Pakistan Times, 27 September 1966.
[49] Dawn, 6 November 1966.
[50] Dawn, 1 December 1966.

The Pakistani leaders were greatly interested in persuading the Soviet Union to stop the supply of arms to India, and Ayub Khan is reported to have raised this matter with Kosygin on his visit to Moscow in September-October 1970. As an alternative, he is said to have pleaded that the Soviet Union should treat Pakistan at par with India in supplying arms. Speaking at a Kremlin banquet, he called "the indiscriminate increase in armaments and the growing military imbalance in the subcontinent a danger to peace."[51]

But the Pakistani President failed in getting his views accepted by the Soviet leaders. They, however, promised him liberal economic aid. In his welcome speech Kosygin again referred to the Tashkent Agreement in the following words:

> The Tashkent meeting confirmed that the road to the solution of existing differences can and must be patiently sought, and the profound community of interests of the peoples which had struggled together against colonialism can be stronger than the differences and contradictions from the past.[52]

The Soviet Union does not want to promote an arms race between India and Pakistan, as it considers this harmful to the economic development of the two countries. It agreed to supply arms to India because of the increased threat to Indian security from the military hardware, valued at 2,000 million dollars, supplied by the USA to Pakistan. The USSR has supplied India with only a reasonable quantity of arms to help meet normal defence requirements, which have acquired a new urgency in the

[51] Keesing's Contemporary Archives, Vol. 16, 1967, p. 22345.
[52] Dawn, 26 September 1967.

light of China's bellicosity.

Early in 1968 the Soviet Union decided to supply SU-7 fighter-bombers to India, and this decision came in for sharp criticism in Pakistan. In April the same year Kosygin visited Pakistan, the first ever visit by a Soviet Prime Minister. The visit took place a few days after Pakistan's note to the USA to the effect that it was not interested in the automatic renewal of the lease of the intelligence base at Badaber, near Peshawar, but the note did not foreclose year-to-year renewal. Kosygin was greeted with slogans like "Give us tanks, not tractors." Under these circumstances the Soviet Union was constrained to give a very limited quantity of arms to Pakistan.[53] But the arms supplied consisted of defensive weapons like helicopters, spare parts for aircraft, some medium tanks and field guns. No sophisticated weapons like supersonic fighters and bombers were supplied. The Pakistani press described this supply as "token." But at the same time Pakistan was promised considerable economic and technical assistance for the construction of a steel mill at Kalabagh, in West Punjab, and an atomic power station at Rooppur in East Pakistan.[54]

During his visit Kosygin underlined the basic premises of Soviet policy towards Pakistan. He said:

The Soviet Union has good normal relations with all

[53] According to Wynfred Joshua and Stephen P. Gibert, the Soviet military aid to Pakistan amounts to $ 5 to $ 10 million only, whereas India has received military aid to the tune of $ 600-700 million. Even Iran and Afghanistan received much larger Soviet military aid than Pakistan, namely, $ 100 million and $ 260 million respectively. (*Arms for the Third World: Soviet Military Aid Diplomacy*, London, 1969, p. 102.)

[54] *Dawn*, 22 April, 1968.

[54] *Dawn*, 22 April 1968.

these [West Asian and South Asian countries] including the close neighbours of Pakistan.... We are strang-
ers to designs for using the relations with one country
to the detriment of its relations with others... to sow
the seeds of discord between the states and peoples
which have freed themselves, to seek to confront each
other is the favourite policy of colonisers. They seek
to pursue it now after they have been thrown away.[55]

Kosygin expressed the hope that India and Pakistan
would resolve their outstanding disputes in the spirit of
the Tashkent Declaration. He also made a brief stopover
in New Delhi on his way to Moscow. Speaking to Indian
newsmen, he categorically stated that Indo-Soviet friendship remained unimpaired.

President Yahya Khan's visit to Moscow in June 1970
did not bring success to Pakistan's search for arms. Instead,
the Soviet Union agreed to increase its assistance for a
steel plant. Moscow again reiterated the Tashkent Declaration in the joint communique signed at the conclu-
sion of the visit. The main accent in the communique was
on economic cooperation. Indeed, there were speculations
that "such a project could conceivably be the basis for a
triangular arrangement, with India supplying some of the
metallurgical, electrical and engineering equipment needed
for the steel plant [in Pakistan] from Heavy Engineering
Corporation and Bharat Heavy Electricals, both of which
are familiar with Soviet designs." According to the
Hindustan Times, such an arrangement would be mutually
beneficial and could also form "the basis for wider regional economic cooperation."[56]

[55] *Dawn*, 18 April 1968.
[56] *Hindustan Times*, 30 June 1970.

Soviet President Nikolai Podgorny welcoming President V. V. Giri on his first state visit to the USSR in September 1970, once again stressed the historic importance of the Tashkent Declaration and held that the "document has not exhausted itself and that the spirit of Tashkent should in our days, too, determine the essence of Pakistani-Indian relations." Podgorny declared:

We wish the friendly peoples of India and Pakistan to continue to follow the way indicated by the Tashkent Declaration, a way which—we are convinced—is in full accord with the national interests of the two countries, and the cause of strengthening peace in Asia and the whole world.[57]

President Giri in his speech stated that India adhered to "the letter and spirit of the Tashkent Declaration and hold it as a model of a charter of good neighbourliness."[58] The Soviet Union is concentrating upon the development of mutually benefical economic ties with both India and Pakistan. Soviet assistance to Pakistan during the third five-year plan period totalled $ 81 million.[59] Besides, in July 1968, the Soviet Union agreed to grant $ 66 million credit to Pakistan for purchase of capital goods.[60] The Trade Agreement for 1970 provided for exchange of goods valued at Rs. 110 million each way.[61] A ten year agreement on collaboration in the peaceful uses of

[57] *Soviet Review*, New Delhi, No. 64, 1970, p. 8.
[58] *Ibid.*, p. 10.
[59] *Keesing's Archives*, 1968, p. 8486.
[60] *Ibid.*
[61] *Ibid.*, 1970, p. 9447.

atomic energy between the Soviet Union and Pakistan was also concluded in 1970. A five year trade agreement is planned to be finalized in 1971.

The Indo-Soviet economic cooperation has maintained its upward trend. From 1955 to 1968, the Soviet Union granted to India eight long term credits valued at nearly Rs 1021 crores. The Soviet aided projects today produce 30% of India's total steel, 35% of oil, 20% of electric power, 60% of heavy electrical equipments, and 80% of heavy machines.[62] The five year Indo-Soviet trade agreement concluded on 26 December 1970 envisages a 75% increase in the next five years. The annual trade plan for 1971 which was simultaneously signed stipulates a 15% increase in trade. By 1975, the level of India's exports to the USSR will rise from Rs 190 crores this year to about Rs 335 crores. The emphasis has been on raising exports of non-traditional goods to the USSR. By 1975, manufactured goods will constitute 60% of India's exports to Russia against 44% at present.[63]

Unlike the United States which menaced peace in Asia by roping in many Asian countries in military pacts, the Soviet accent has been on non-military means of strengthening peace in this area through close regional economic cooperation. It was in line with this approach that Brezhnev suggested the idea of an Asian Collective Security System in his address to the World Communist Conference in June 1969. A few weeks earlier, during his visit to Kabul, Kosygin proposed regional economic and trade cooperation involving India, Pakistan, Afghanis-

[62] K. N. Aiyar, "Indo-Soviet Economic Relations: A Review", A paper submitted at the Seminar on Indo-Soviet Relations, New Delhi, 8 November 1970.
[63] Times of India, 27 December 1970.

tan, Iran, and Turkey. The details of the idea of Asian Security System have been implicitly left to be worked out by the Asian countries themselves. In his speech at Alma Ata, Brezhnev categorically denied that the proposed Asian Collective Security System was aimed against China.[64] According to *Shakai Shimpo*, official organ of the Japanese Socialist Party, the Soviet Communist Party theoritician, Suslov, told a visiting Japanese delegation that the proposed security system has to be preceded by US withdrawal from Vietnam, and disengagement of Asian nations from all military pacts.[65]

Good neighbourly relations between India and Pakistan—two of the most powerful countries of the region—are viewed by the Soviet Union as the sheet anchor of Asian security.[66] Having achieved considerable success towards detente in Europe recently, the Soviet Union is eagei to improve the political climate in an area with preponderant majority of the world's population.

Right from the very beginning, Soviet policy towards India and Pakistan has been consistently aimed at strengthening friendship with both, while trying to bring them closer to each other. This is a part of Soviet Union's general policy of befriending all countries, especially its neighbours, without prejudicing their relations or Soviet relations with other countries.

[64] *Soviet Review*, New Delhi, No. 60, 1970, p. 25.
[65] *Far Eastern Economic Review*, 17 October 1970, p. 37.
[66] *Pravda*, 28 June 1970.

INDEX

ABDURAB, leader of the Indian revolutionary Association in Tashkent, 16

Afghanistan, relation with Soviet Union, 59, 74; Brezhnev visit to, 110

All-India Students' Federation Conference, Soviet delegation to, 28

All-India Trade Union Congress, 22

Alma Ata, Brezhnev's at, 111

Anglo-American bloc, 35

Anglo-American countries, 28

Anglo-American Imperialism, 33

Anglo-Russian rivalry, 5

Anglo-Russian Trade Agreement of March 1921, 20-21

Asian Collective Security System, Brezhnev's Address to the World Communist Conference, 110

Astra Khan, Colony of Indians, Indian trade in, 3

Atlantic Charter, Churchill's declaration about the non-applicability of, 24

Austrian Neutrality, signing the treaty of, 53

Avanti, 34

Avarin, V., 61

Ayub, Mohammed, 81

BADABER (near Peshwar), intelligence base at, 107

Baghdad Pact, Khrushchev's views on Pakistan's Membership of, 59

Balabushevich, V. V., 15, 33

Bandung Conference, 54, 77; principles of, 89

Banerjea, Surendranath, 3

Belgrade, Nehru's visit to, 56

Belyaev, I., 91

Benedictov, I. A, visit to Pakistan, 77

Bhagavatgita, The, 2

Bhandarkar, R. G., 3

Bhilai Steel Plant, 49, 66-67

Bhutto, Z. A., 79, 89; criticism of Tashkent Declaration, 100

Black Sea Coast, 1

Bolsheviks, Address by, 10-11

Bombay, visit of Russian Warship to, 7

Bourgeois Nationalist Movement, 11-12

Brezhnev, 69, 90-91; support the Indian Government's action in Goa, 71; visit to Afghanistan, Iran, Turkey, 110

"Brezhnev-Kosygin team", 81

British Commonwealth of Nations, continuation in, 28

Buddhism, 2

Budhraj, 32

Bukhara, Centre of trade and communication with India, 4

Bulganin, 51, 55-56; admiration for Gandhi's leadership, 60;